ENERGY, THE FLIP SIDE OF MONEY

ENERGY, THE FLIP SIDE OF MONEY

Typesetting : Konsensus Network

Cover design artwork by Miron Schmückle

Edited by: Mel Shilling

ISBN 978-9916-749-63-0 Hardcover

978-9916-749-64-7 Paperback

Konsensus Network ★ https://konsensus.network

Foreword

This book is dedicated to all the scientists who, through their often painstaking research and sometimes brilliant discoveries, provide us with the keys to understanding our environment with a clarity unmatched in the history of humanity.

I would also like to thank the people whose outstanding work helped me bring this project to completion: Schuler Goepfert, Edouard Gallego, Mel Shilling, Josefina Alonso and Miron Schmuckle.

Writing is an all-consuming mistress, yet it reduces the author's entropy by forcing them to organize their knowledge.

"An author writes from a lookout where he watches himself live. He is absent from the world and, paradoxically, closer to the core of existence."

– Emma Becker

Contents

Intro

Every time you swipe through social media, you tap into vast networks of servers consuming megawatts of electricity. When you order takeout, you initiate a chain of energy transfers – from the farm machinery that harvested the ingredients, to the trucks that transported them, to the ovens that cooked your meal, to the scooter or car that delivers it to your door. Even as you read these words, your brain consumes glucose, converting chemical energy into the electrical impulses that create thought and consciousness.

These everyday actions reveal a fundamental pattern of nature - the constant flow and transformation of energy. This pattern governs more than our phones, vehicles, and bodies; it also describes our societies, economies, and even our behavior as human beings.

The science behind this pattern – particularly the third law of thermodynamics – offers a powerful lens for understanding the major challenges of our century, such as climate change, migration, and inequality. These issues often spark heated ideological debates, but viewing them through the framework of energy reveals surprising insights about how our world really works. This work explores how the physical principles of energy influence our social behaviors and shape our economic incentives. It leads us beyond polarized arguments and toward more rational discussions at a time when extreme beliefs and dogmas seem to dominate public discourse.

This book is not the first to recognize energy's central role in human development. *The Evolution of Culture*, by American anthropologist Leslie White, interprets the history of humanity through the extraction of energy from its environment. Initially, hunter-gatherers captured only the chemical energy of their food. Later, farmers learned to capture solar energy through agriculture and mechanical energy through animal husbandry, allowing them to convert animal power into mechanical work. Finally, humans learned to extract energy from increasingly complex non-biological dissipative structures: fuels, metals, machines, and nuclear energy.

Cultural evolution accompanied this movement. As we developed new ways to harness energy, we evolved innovative ways of organizing ourselves and passing knowledge between generations. Our species demonstrates its self-organization around the transmission of collective behaviors beyond genes. In all cases, whether the evolution was Darwinian or cultural, the selected behaviors were intended to maximize energy capture.

My research also led me to discover Ernst Haeckel (1834-1919), a German scientist and free thinker whose insights resonate deeply with this book's themes. His understanding of the theory of evolution, which I connect to the third law of thermodynamics, allowed him to disseminate these revolutionary ideas at a time when they were still highly controversial.

In Haeckel's naturalist philosophy, the world was explained not by the hypothesis of the divine but by a single, natural, and immanent principle. He had insight into the unity of the substance that composes the universe and living beings. Advancements in physics in the 20th century would confirm this unity, identifying it as energy.

His controversial side, pan-Germanist and supremacist, does not deter me from appreciating other ideas he developed. This is also a stance taken in this book: to discuss the merits of an idea rather than the qualities of the person who expressed it. Reason shouldn't be discredited simply because its messenger may have been wrong about other things.

Despite the impressive amount of scientific and philosophical literature on energy, there remains the need to explain the crucial link between energy, information, and currency.

I was driven to write about this subject because the tyranny of emotions increasingly drowns out rationality in public debate in many areas, particularly in economics and ecology. The importance of the issues attracts demagogues and censors to controversies, where it becomes difficult to untangle truth from falsehood.

This essay offers the foundations for a scientific and anthropological approach to a coherent monetary and environmental policy. It does not judge the degrowth advocates, Keynesians, or crypto-anarchists but outlines the calm conversation they could have.

By addressing energy and information, this book aims to move beyond the chatter and confusion surrounding monetary systems, whether they are state-run, monopolistic, or decentralized, whose fundamentals are too often ignored. It offers more than just a line of thought: a dharma in the Buddhist sense of the term. That is, a framework for understanding the world and the forces that govern it.

For believers in the divine hypothesis, these forces are transcendent. For the skeptic that I have become, they result from the immanent principles that govern energy and reveal it as the essence of all things.

In this book, I use the Taoist symbolism of Yin and Yang to describe the polarity of energy flows - from the dynamics of seduction to the tension between the need for freedom (Yang) and the need for security (Yin). I use Yin and Yang as mathematical symbols without associating them with any belief. Yin and Yang represent sets of complementary concepts, such as competition and cooperation or masculine and feminine.

Energy's special role in nature explains how it profoundly shapes our existence – our desire to learn and create, to believe and dream, to order and liberate, as well as many other behaviors that may appear inconsistent or contradictory. Even Darwinian evolution, economic crises, and climate change can be analyzed through the science of energy.

Using the three principles of thermodynamics as our foundation, we will explore how energy and information interact through concrete examples developed in various chapters.

This essay is not consensual. It escapes a homogeneous labeling of its chapters among libertarian, progressive, or ecological pathways, or what have you. The application of thermodynamics to economics or anthropology introduces a certain determinism, a connection to reality that challenges ideological approaches.

Tempered by the complexity of living beings, this determinism contrasts with the elegant simplicity of the first causes revealed by science. The science of energy allows us to correctly define what physical quantities should be optimized in the economic field, something traditional economics and monetary policy, with their focus on interest rates, price inflation, and taxation, often fail to do.

We see this same limitation in contemporary philosophy. The French intelligentsia (Sartre, Deleuze, Derrida, Foucault), ignoring the fundamentals of energy, often descend into verbosity. Yet, the philosopher Jacques Bouveresse not only denounced this flaw but also proved through the wisdom of his writings on entropy that such verbal excess is not inevitable, provided one has the intelligence and the will to work on the subject.

Significant breakthroughs, whether in the arts or sciences, often require bridging the gaps between multiple disciplines. Consider Nicola Salvi, the architect of the Trevi Fountain in Rome, who studied painting, philosophy, mathematics, and architecture. Or Henri Poincaré, the inventor of chaos theory and the theory of special relativity (wrongly attributed to the author of general relativity, Einstein). Such polymaths[1] show us what is possible when we transcend artificial academic partitions of knowledge.

A human society can be compared to a network where the nodes are individuals. To maximize their energy flow, individuals can follow two paths (two "taos"): conquest or adaptation. Conquest seeks to capture more energy from the environment, like building a dam to harness a river's power. Adaptation, by contrast, optimizes the physical and cognitive abilities to facilitate that capture, like developing more efficient farming techniques.

These paths embody the essential duality of Yang and Yin. They aren't mutually exclusive, and each individual possesses both as complementary forces, meaning we can adapt to our environment while simultaneously seeking to shape it.

In this work, we will explore at least nine fundamental concepts that reveal how energy functions in our universe:

1. **The Principle of Conservation**: Energy does not disappear; it transforms.
2. **Energy Flows and Reserves**: Energy exists as either reserves (stocks) or flows. Think of reserves as nature's batteries: particles, molecules, materials, objects, and living beings store potential energy, chemical energy, nuclear energy, etc. Flows are energy in motion: electrical currents, objects in motion (kinetic energy), machines doing work (mechanical energy) work, etc. So-called renewable energy sources are flows, such as wind, hydraulic, or solar energy.
3. **Renewable Energy**: Renewable energies – wind, hydraulic, solar – are *flows* of energy. The transformation of a renewable energy flow generates temporary shortages or surpluses because variations in demand are not synchronized with the inherently intermittent flow. Batteries can store a flow of electrical energy, and thus a portion of the surpluses, in the form of chemical energy.
4. **Fossil Energy**: Fossil energies are *reserves* of energy. Oil and coal experience virtually no surpluses because the use of a reserve can be deferred when demand decreases.
5. **Free Energy**: Free energy is energy that is easy to use and particularly easy to convert into mechanical work. For example, electrical energy is a form of free energy because it can be efficiently converted into mechanical energy by an electric motor.
6. **Heat**: Heat is a degraded form of energy. It's diffused and difficult to convert into free energy.
7. **The Vacuum**: Far from empty nothingness, the vacuum contains energy flows, is a source of matter (and antimatter), and is the site of fundamental interactions.
8. **Space**: Space has neither center nor boundary, and time has neither beginning nor end.

9. **Dissipative Structures**: Energy concentrates in the form of dissipative structures, and every dissipative structure self-organizes in turn to maximize the flow of energy it captures. The term "dissipative structures" refers to all observable systems nested within one another in a succession that starts from elementary particles to the universe, passing through atoms, molecules, living beings, species, planets, etc.

This nesting structure of energy reveals itself everywhere - from the branching patterns in the tree of life to the organized layers of the periodic table of elements. It reflects how the random movements of energy concentrate in increasingly complex forms. Like cosmic dances, phases of energy concentration follow periods of diffusion in a perpetual cycle. These oscillations can be observed, for example, during mass extinctions of species followed by a new phase of living expansion. Stars, too, follow this pattern. They are born, concentrate energy for billions of years, and then die in spectacular releases of energy.

The process of maximizing energy flow at the scale of each structure creates self-organizing, interdependent patterns. Each living species self-organizes through the reproduction of individuals and the evolution of their physical or cognitive abilities.

Some insects spend ten years of their lives in the larval state and only a few months as adults. In this case, we can say that the dissipative structure is self-organized around the reproduction and multiplication of the members of the species (Yin). The human species, more aligned with Yang , self-organizes around the maximization of the flow captured by the individual and the accumulation of knowledge.

The interconnection of dissipative structures works in multiple directions. They flow vertically, from one scale to another, such as between fish and the ocean, and also horizontally, from one branch of life to another, such as between birds and plants.

To illustrate the individual-species interconnection inherent to the third principle of thermodynamics, the behavior of a tree as a dissipative structure is very telling. Early in its life, the tree initially devotes all its energy to growth in order to reach adulthood. Once grown, it then captures a maximum amount of energy and thus shifts energy to reproduction, which contributes to the evolution of the species. The species self-organizes in this way to adapt to its environment through natural selection and give birth to individuals who will capture even more energy.

Like any dissipative structure, the human species is doomed to extinction and can only try to delay it. The sun provides a steady energy source for the next four billion years, a timeline that may seem like an ambitious survival goal. Following Gramsci's recommendation, I try to temper the pessimism of intelligence with the optimism of will: we can do it. The disenchantment of the world through progress is not a melancholy of magical thinking. It calls us to embrace the nobility of the human condition in the rationality and wonder of discovery.

Part 1: What is Energy?

1. Principle of Conservation

"Nothing is lost, nothing is created, everything is transformed."

This statement, inspired by Lavoisier, remains the clearest and most precise description: the "nothing" here is also the "everything," that is, energy, invisible but omnipresent.

Lavoisier first expressed the conservation of mass as early as 1789. Two centuries later, Einstein's special relativity demonstrated that mass and energy are linked, making the conservation of mass a particular case of the conservation of energy.

This principle extends beyond physics. In economics, for example, the monetary concept of a country's gross domestic product (GDP) is a measure of the amount of energy used by the residents of that country.

Specifically, GDP is the value of national production minus intermediate consumption. It is measured from the expenditure perspective by summing all expenditures for consumption or wealth creation, adding exports, and subtracting imports of goods and services. Because the creation of wealth corresponds to energy saved or additional energy released, real GDP (measured at constant prices) and the amount of energy dissipated are in a proportional relationship, as illustrated in this graph.

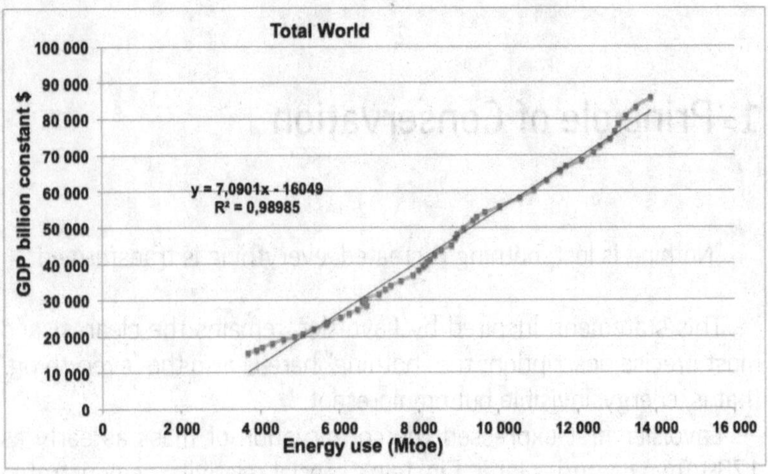

Source : The Shift Project

This principle of conservation—the first principle of thermodynamics—implies that any open system, exchanging energy with its surroundings, is an energy converter. In other words, it is a dissipative structure that receives energy and transforms part of it into free energy (a form of reusable energy) and another part into heat.

2. Second Principle

"Without energy exchange with the outside, the energy of a system tends to disperse as much as possible."

This first rigorous formulation was formulation of the second principle is generally attributed to the German physicist Rudolf Clausius (1822-1888), inspired by the work of Nicolas Léonard Sadi Carnot. This French physicist Carnot Considered, the founder of thermodynamics, French physicist Carnot demonstrated as early as 1824 that it is impossible to produce motive power without having both a cold body and a hot body. Embodying that simplicity does not detract from depth, Clausius later summarized this principle:

"Heat always passes from a warmer body to a cooler one." Clausius introduced the concept of entropy in 1865 to characterize the microscopic disorder of a system, its degree of disorganization.

Entropy accounts for the degree of energy dispersion (thermal, chemical, etc.) within the system itself. In other words, the second law of thermodynamics states that in an isolated system – one that exchanges neither work nor heat with its surroundings –tends to increase to reach a maximum value where the system remains in equilibrium.

The concept of entropy is even more abstract than that of energy. It appears across multiple disciplines, from physics (thermodynamics) to various branches of mathematics (information theory, probability theory).

In thermodynamics, entropy measures the level of disorder of a system for a given observer. In other words, the entropy of a system measures the hidden information within the system. A low-entropy system is ordered and predictable, while a high-entropy system is disorganized and chaotic. Like velocity, which changes depending on the observer's frame of reference, entropy is a relative notion since the amount of hidden information depends on the amount of prior information collected by the observer.

In mathematics, entropy quantifies uncertainty in dynamic systems, such as sequences of numbers in random processes. In information theory, entropy refers to the amount of information contained in a data source. High entropy means that the data source can take many different states and generates information that is difficult to predict. Low entropy, means, on the other hand, indicates that the messages present few possible states.

Entropy is also used in probability theory to measure the heterogeneity of a probability distribution. High entropy means that the probabilities of different events are similar and do not indicate a clear trend. Low entropy, on the other hand, means that some events have a much higher probability than others.

The first and second principles allow us to distinguish energy from entropy because entropy is not conserved. Indeed, information can reduce the entropy of its recipient. However, information can replicate and spread to multiple observers. Since it reduces the entropy of all these observers, information behaves like a quantity of negative entropy, which is incompatible with the conservation of entropy.

According to the second principle, a closed system receiving neither information nor energy will sees its entropy increase. The first principle states that energy is conserved in quantity, and the second tells us that it degrades in quality.

To gain an understanding of what entropy represents, let's take, as an observed system, an isothermal container with two compartments and 10 molecules of gas in the left compartment.

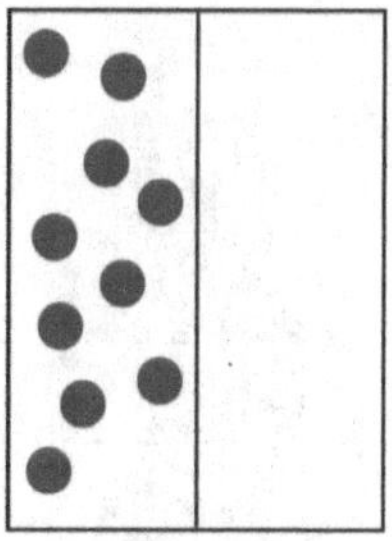

The two compartments are separated by a mesh covered by a solid sheet of metal. If we now lift the metal barrier in the middle, the mesh will let particles spread out through the entire box.

The second principle tells us that gas molecules are more likely to pass through the perforations from the left to the right side than in the reverse. Initially, we can predict the movement of gas molecules through the mesh with high probability. But, once the gas has diffused into the entire box, the observer's uncertainty increases: molecular movement between compartments becomes random and unpredictable. Entropy is at its maximum.

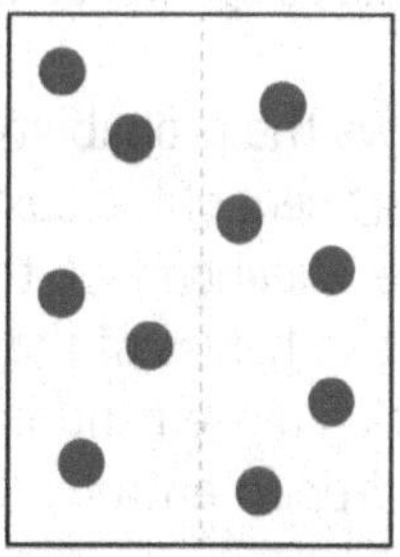

Why is it so ? It's get interesting when we try to find an explanation to this fundamental law of nature: the reason has to do with probability theory. To get a grasp of what's going on here, imagine now we have only 4 particles, to keep things simple, and there are only 4 slots as possible positions for them in each compartment of our box.

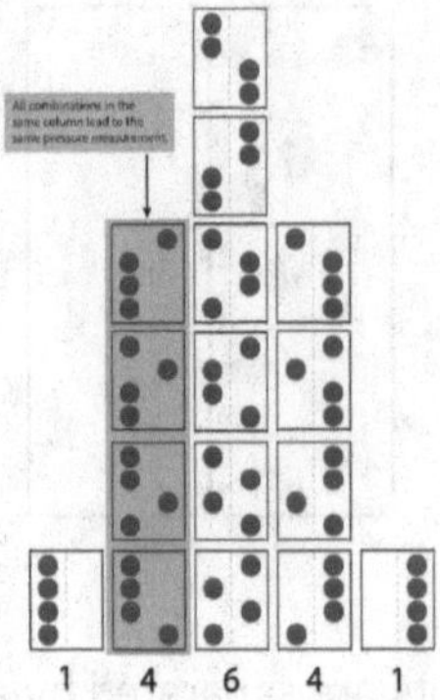

As illustrated above, in this simplified situation, our 4 particles have only one possible state if they are all in one compartment but 4 possible states if one of them escapes to the other side and 6 possible states to be evenly distributed with 2 particles on each side of the box. In other words, if particles are moving randomly, they are much more likely to move towards a state of maximum entropy than to stay nicely arranged in only one compartment of the box. And if that is true for our simplified 4 particle model, the predicition is even more relevant for a large number of particles.

The chances of all particles spontaneously gathering in one corner become very tiny.

The curve below shows the probability of finding x out of 1000 particles in the left compartment of the box. There is a clear maximum around 500, that is the likelihood of the particles being evenly distributed between the two halves of the box.

Because of the brownian movement of the particles, there can be an occasional and local drop in entropy, but it cannot last or grow statiscally speaking.

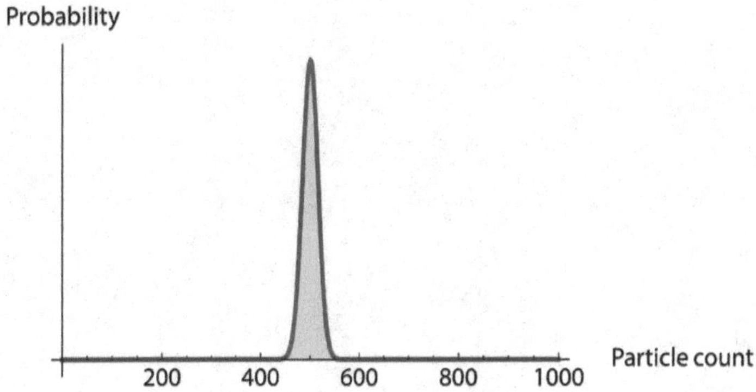

Probability of seeing X particles in one of the halves. 500 particles are the most likely by far and deviations become vastly more unlikely the larger they are.

Because we are complex dissipative structures made of billions of atoms, the chances of a lasting decrease in entropy are very slim. We are made of 10 000 billion cells. There is no practical way to reverse the arrow of time and undo the process of aging, the gradual increase of the entropy of the particles we are made of.

At the other end of the complexity spectrum, a molecule of water, as a very stable arrangement of 3 atoms, is almost eternal. The first water molecules go as far back as the aftermath of the Big Bang, almost 14 billion years ago. Time does not really exist for a molecule of water.

3. Third Principle

"Every dissipative structure self-organizes to maximize the flow of the energy it captures."

This profound insight earned Ilya Prigogine (1917-2003), a Belgian physicist of Russian origin, the Nobel Prize in Chemistry in 1977. His seminal 1960 paper introduced the concept of irreversible process thermodynamics, launching an entirely new field of study.

Our initial understanding evolved through several key contributions. Per Bak (1948-2002) first formulated the concept of self-organized criticality in 1987. Later, Roderick Dewar's 2002 publication on the fluctuation-dissipation theorem linked self-organized criticality to the third principle. The third principle thus synthesizes works stretching from Boltzmann and Josiah Willard Gibbs' pioneering studies of entropy (*Elementary Principles in Statistical Physics*, 1902), continuing with those of Claude Shannon (the father of information theory) and Jaynes.

At this point, it is helpful to clarify a debate around the designation of this third principle. It is often referred to as the principle of maximum entropy production, the principle of maximization of energy dissipation, and sometimes even the principle of minimization of entropy production. To add to the confusion, historically, the third principle referred to something quite different – Walther Hermann Nernst's 1920 Nobel Prize-winning discovery that any pure substance in a perfect crystalline state has zero entropy at absolute zero (0) Kelvin.

In reality, Nernst's principle has little to do with that of Prigogine and is more closely related to the second principle in reverse: if the entropy of a closed system tends to a maximum, there is also a minimum that corresponds to zero entropy, which allows for a determined value of entropy rather than an approximate value with an additive constant.

Prigogine's principle states that when only one stationary state is possible, the system evolves towards a stationary state that minimizes entropy production. It remains to clarify the principle of Maximum Entropy Production (abbreviated as MEP). This principle stipulates that a non-equilibrium system in a stationary state aims for a final state that maximizes entropy production. Think of a living being or a flag as an example of non-equilibrium systems. Without sustenance, the living being dies; without wind, the flag falls limp. These open systems exist out of equilibrium, requiring external energy to maintain their stationary states.

The principle of maximum entropy production states that an open system will evolve, among all possible stationary states, towards the one that maximizes the production of entropy.

In other words, if the thermodynamic forces are fixed, then the thermodynamic flows self-organize to maximize entropy production. For example, water follows the line of greatest slope to dissipate its gravitational potential energy to the maximum.

Because it governs the dynamics of entropy, the principle of maximum entropy production complements the second principle, which predicts its final state, namely maximum entropy.

Let us now examine the opening statement about energy capture. The captured energy flow is also a partially dissipated energy flow, with dissipation here meaning the partial transformation of energy into heat, hence the term dissipative structure. We should understand these structures as "energy converters" in a broad sense.

A bicycle converts the flow of mechanical energy provided by the cyclist into kinetic energy. This is its purpose. When the flow stops, the bicycle stops and can fall. When the flow of chemical energy contained in the cyclist's food is interrupted, he can die of starvation. The bicycle and the cyclist are thus dissipative structures.

A dissipative structure stores some captured energy, converts some to free energy flow, and dissipates the rest as heat. In some cases, the dissipation is almost total, as in the conversion of electrical energy into heat by a heating appliance. In others, dissipation is minimal, such as in the transformation of electrical energy into mechanical energy by a motor. In all cases, the transfer of heat outside the open system corresponds to entropy production. Our statement on energy capture thus parallels the principle of maximum entropy production.

As we noted with the second principle, heat is a form of diffuse energy that is difficult to convert into another form of energy. Free energy is, by definition, an energy directly convertible into mechanical energy.

Entropy (and, therefore, information, negative entropy) links time and energy. Money is a very special kind of information because it is the closest to what it represents, this being energy and time. People considered rich generally have more "free" time (note how this expression echoes free energy) than others. Free time is not synonymous with idleness but with optionality, meaning the ability to choose what to do with this time.

Free time is precious precisely because it is rare. Time spent capturing vital, homeostatic energy is not "free." If we lived indefinitely, it would become impossible to prioritize our activities. Given infinite time, we would necessarily experience all possible states and situations – unless remaining forever immobile (our definition of death) or circling within a finite loop of activities (defining boredom or even hell).

Time (T) and energy (E) are connected by the concept of power (P) with the formula $\mathbf{E = P \times T}$.

We can state the third principle by emphasizing that a dissipative structure self-organizes to maximize its power since the measure of the energy flow passing through it is precisely the structure's power. For a non-biological dissipative structure like a car, performance optimization comes through a living structure, its designer. The self-organization of the designer-machine pair benefits both the designer-user and the machine in return, creating a virtuous circle.

In reality, every open system is a dissipative structure because energy itself recursively self-organizes in the form of dissipative structures. A dissipative structure can thus refer to a primary level of energy condensation, such as an elementary particle, an atom, a molecule, a living being, a planet, or even a complete universe.

This local condensation of energy in the form of dissipative structures reflects the fluctuations of energy, which concentrates in order to better diffuse itself. The self-organization of a dissipative structure involves an internal reduction of entropy, which enables it to receive a greater energy flow.

The third principle deals with maximum entropy production because any increase in the incoming energy flow is accompanied by an increase in dissipation, even if this dissipation is sometimes relatively low, as in the case of an electric motor. When the dissipated energy is at its maximum, the structure gradually fades out or abruptly explodes, and dissipation consequently decreases.

For example, a predator reduces its entropy by accumulating information about its prey, which allows it to capture more and increase the flow of chemical energy that constitutes its diet. By acquiring information, the predator reduces its own entropy level while making the prey's environment more uncertain. Consequently, the predator increases the entropy of its prey both through accumulated information and additional energy capture.

In summary, a dissipative structure maximizes its energy capture by reducing its internal entropy as part of an optimization strategy and by exporting entropy externally as part of a conquest strategy.

Having outlined the three principles, we will now explore the foundational concepts of energy and entropy in greater depth. Finally, we will demonstrate, through concrete examples, how these principles and abstract ideas manifest in our world, shaping the forces of nature and governing the behaviors of physical systems.

4. Energy

Why write about energy? It is both an abstraction and a universal, physical reality with concrete effects. Its invisible power evokes fears, and its utility arouses desires, so much so that it has become a political bargaining chip exploited by parties that claim to be environmentalists. Reason must find its place again in debates on this subject, often dominated by fears.

The drawbacks of a particular energy source can only be analyzed in relation to existing alternatives such as wind turbines, solar panels, power plants, or nuclear energy. However, there is peculiar hypervigilance concerning nuclear energy, contrasted with a relative blindness to the consequences of abandoning it.

Ironically, the fear of nuclear energy kills more than nuclear energy itself. In March 2011, following the emotion caused by the Fukushima disaster in Japan, Germany decided to phase out nuclear energy. This decision forced the country to restart its coal-fired power plants, which emit harmful particulates. However, it turns out that the health impact of pollution from fine particles is considerable, with an estimated 48,000 deaths per year in France. It also reduced life expectancy by at least two years for those aged 30, according to a 2016 study by Santé Publique France.[2]

In a striking contrast, the radioactive fallout from the Fukushima accident caused no direct deaths, and even ten years after the event, no cases of cancer could be attributed to the incident's radioactive fallout. This data is confirmed in the report by UNSCEAR, a UN scientific committee established in 1955 that operates on a model similar to the IPCC for climate.

The Cold War taught us to accept smaller localized wars to avoid a great world war. Similarly, choosing nuclear energy means preferring manageable local disasters (Three Mile Island, Chernobyl, Fukushima) rather than an uncontrollable global catastrophe, i.e., climate change. This trade-off appears rational, though it must remain open to debate, as all decisions involving public power should.

Even hydroelectric power, as pure and harmless as it may seem, has proven far more dangerous to local populations than any nuclear power plant in cases of mismanagement or dam failures. For example, the Malpasset dam disaster in 1959 claimed 423 lives, yet it has been overshadowed in public memory by less lethal nuclear accidents.

Renewable energy alternatives are often promoted by private entrepreneurs whose communication strategies far outshine those of public entities, the only institution capable of advancing the nuclear industry today.

We must, therefore, be wary of hasty conclusions, false intuitions, and preconceived notions about energy. Firstly, we must understand how it works. As the novelist Ayn Rand wrote in *The Objectivists Ethics* (1961), "Man is free to evade reality, he is free to unfocus his mind and stumble blindly down any road he pleases, but not free to avoid the abyss he refuses to see. Man is free to choose not to be conscious, but not free to escape the penalty of unconsciousness: destruction."

Writing about energy brings to mind philosophers who conceived of God as the sole substance and cause of everything. Consider this passage from Baruch Spinoza's *Ethics*: "Everything that is, is in God, and nothing can be or be conceived without God." Replace "God" with "energy," and the statement remains strikingly similar.

By denouncing anthropomorphism – the attribution of human objectives or emotions to God (God "loves" the humans he created) – Spinoza makes God practically indistinguishable from the structuring, limitless, and ubiquitous force that is energy. The primary mystery lies less in the emergence of life but more in the principles of how energy functions. For believers, God can remain the great architect who conceived these rules, but this conception is far removed from the deity described in sacred texts.

The concept of energy, whose level of abstraction is matched only by the power of its manifestations in the tangible world, has developed alongside the language of mathematics. Mathematics translates abstract thoughts into symbols, reasoning into sequences of symbols, and conclusions into formulas.

According to my physics professor at the École Polytechnique, Roger Balian, in his article "The Long Elaboration of the Concept of Energy," mathematician Joseph-Louis Lagrange introduced the concept of mechanical energy in his 1788 work, *Mécanique Analytique*, expanding it beyond the realms of dynamics and forces.

Later, the mathematician David Hilbert (1862-1943) laid the groundwork for quantum mechanics. Balian credits Hermann von Helmholtz, a Prussian physician (1821-1892), with defining the general concept of energy, discovering that "transformations of matter translate into changes in the nature of energy, and that its total value remains conserved," thus confirming the Lavoisier's principle of conservation from a century earlier.

Helmholtz was also preceded by Ludvig Colding, a Danish physicist (1815-1888), who in 1843 envisioned "energy as the essence of things, an entity underlying matter."

By establishing an equivalence between mass and energy, Einstein's famous equation, $E = mc^2$, contributed to a progressive generalization of the concept of energy over the past two centuries. If matter is condensed energy, it can be released in multiple ways. For example, when a deuterium nucleus and a tritium nucleus meet to fuse into a helium nucleus, the mass of the product is less than the sum of the masses of the fused nuclei. The difference is transformed into energy according to Einstein's formula.

Free Energy

Free energy is defined as a form of energy that is easily usable, meaning it can be readily converted into work, another form of free energy, or useful heat. Examples include chemical energy, electrical energy, potential energy, and kinetic energy.

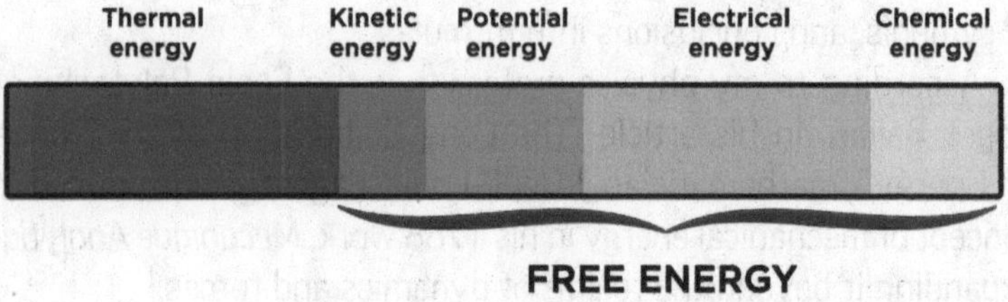

Free Energy spectrum

Chemical Energy

Food provides this energy to living beings. Fossil fuels, such as oil, are reserves of chemical energy that release useful heat through combustion, a chemical reaction with oxygen.

Electrical Energy

Electric current is easily convertible into mechanical energy by a motor. The inverse conversion is done by a dynamo, which uses mechanical energy to convert it into electricity.

Potential Energy

Reaching the top of a pass, a cyclist has accumulated gravitational potential energy by pedaling. They can recover this store of potential energy as a flow of kinetic energy during the descent.

Kinetic Energy

This is the energy that a body possesses due to its motion relative to a reference frame. Its value depends on the selected reference frame.

Thermal Energy

Commonly referred to as heat, this energy represents what remains when free energy is no longer available, according to the principle of conservation.

Energy, measured in joules (J), is named after English physicist James Prescott Joule, who discovered the formula for calculating the heat dissipated by a resistor when an electric current passes through it. The amount of energy can also be expressed in watt-hours (Wh), where one watt-hour equals 3,600 joules. The watt, the unit of physical power, is a flow of energy and is equivalent to one joule per second. This unit, along with its multiples – mega (MWh, one million), giga (GWh, one billion), or tera (TWh, one trillion)–is commonly used to quantify energy.

Photosynthesis: Example of Energy Conversion

Plants convert light energy into chemical energy. Using light, they combine carbon dioxide (CO_2) from the atmosphere with water (H_2O) absorbed through their roots to synthesize glucose ($C_6H_{12}O_6$), releasing oxygen (O_2) in the process. Sometimes, the plant produces more energy than it needs, releasing excess glucose through its roots.

What is a Dissipative Structure?

This term, central to the third principle, simply refers to an open system that receives energy and partially converts it into free energy, with the rest transformed into heat. Dissipation characterizes the transformation of energy into heat, a diffuse form of energy that is difficult to use.

A truly closed system exists only in laboratories or thought experiments, as perfectly isolating a system from all energy exchanges is practically impossible.

The Third Principle and the Living World

According to the third principle, living beings are complex dissipative structures that self-organize to capture as much energy as possible, beginning with the chemical energy from food. Since dissipative structures are interconnected, they are part of larger structures, such as species, which also behave as converters.

A species maximizes energy capture in two ways: by increasing its population through reproduction and by optimizing individual energy capture through evolution. Evolution requires the cycle of birth and death that characterizes living beings. Without death as an essential corollary of evolution, overpopulation would impose the law of diminishing returns[3] on the maximization process.

In the absence of a life-death cycle, the population of the species would quickly increase to the point where the species has no more incentive as a dissipative structure to optimize individual energy capture by Darwinian evolution, since population growth alone would ensure an increasing amount of energy would be captured by the species as a whole. But the limited availability of energy sources and raw materials would mean the law of diminishing returns applies.

Without death, without birth, the species becomes static, and, again, the only way it can increase energy capture is by building machines and exploiting new energy sources.

With evolution, the species as a dissipative structure can become more complex, and its evolution becomes less predictable. It reduces its entropy by exporting part of it to its environment. Increasing complexity allows energy to explore a greater diversity of possible paths, as shown by the representation of evolution in the form of the tree of life.

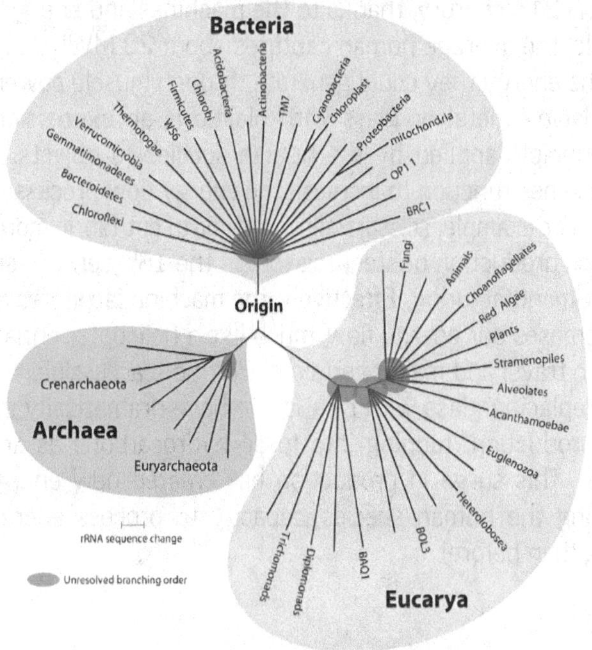

By integrating the cycle of birth and death, the principle of self-organization has given rise to the phenomenon of homeostasis, where multiple reactions come into play, and their effects balance each other to maintain a dynamic equilibrium. In other words, homeostasis is the ability of an organism to maintain a relative constancy of its internal environment in response to external disturbances.

Homeostasis emerges with complexity. It is a form of self-organization oriented towards increasing duration (to integrate more energy over time), rather than increasing power. As life evolves toward greater complexity, its physical and cognitive abilities expand, enabling it to capture more energy.

These abilities increase not only through genetic evolution but also through the creation of machines – boats, trains, cars, planes, robots, and other exoskeletons – that serve as secondary converters, amplifying the superior converter that is their creator to multiply their energy capture.

In the 21st century, thanks to the machines and energy sources available, the average human captures about 20 MWh per year, 35 times the energy they could generate through muscle power alone.

Replacing metal or glass with plastic is an expression of the third principle applied by the human species to objects. Objects and machines function to increase the energy flow processed by the species. For example, scissors allow a tailor to cut fabric more quickly. The mass production of steel scissors in the 18th century simplified clothing manufacturing. Effectively, the machine facilitates an action that increases our energy flow, much like a helicopter enhances our ability to travel and makes certain places more accessible.

By replacing glass with plastic, we have dramatically increased bottle production, tapping into fossil hydrocarbons as an energy reserve. This surge in production has created new energy flows, furthering the human species' capacity to process energy (more bottling than before).

5. Entropy

Entropy measures the degree of dispersion of energy in space and time, reflecting the degree of uncertainty an observer has about their environment.

The feeling of well-being in humans is linked to a reduction in entropy. To achieve this, some will learn to understand and form connections with others. They may also explore, experiment, and share their knowledge about their environment. However, per the second principle of thermodynamics, reducing entropy requires an input of energy.

When the entropy of a system increases, the observer loses information about the evolution of this system. This concept links the two other fundamental concepts: energy and information.

Intriguingly, the Buddhist symbolism of the three jewels – Buddha, Dharma, and Sangha – echoes this trio of information, entropy, and energy. Buddha is the source of information, the Dharma represents the principles that reduce entropy, and the Sangha is the energy derived from the community of practitioners.

Entropy and Information

In information theory, pioneered by the American mathematician Claude Shannon in the 1950s, the amount of information contained in a message depends on its probability. For Shannon, entropy is defined as a lack of information. A weather report predicting rain in London contains less information than a similar forecast for the Sahara Desert. Note that the entropy of an information source is zero when there is no uncertainty, e.g., if the source always emits the same message.

This reveals a fundamental property of information and entropy: their value depends on the observer, the one who receives the information, in a context that is unique to them.

Mathematician and physicist John von Neumann quipped, "Nobody really knows what entropy is." Nevertheless, let's try to illustrate the concept through sensation and perception. Sensation is the capture of information by the senses, information fragmented by the diversity of entry points, at a minimum, through the five senses. Perception, on the other hand, is a reduction of entropy by synthesizing the information. The information is sorted, ordered, and prioritized, thus becoming usable to release or save a certain amount of energy.

Buddhist thought aligns with this distinction and has long noted the importance of this distinction between sensation and perception. Samadhi, an intermediate state of concentration induced by meditation, places us between perception and non-perception. The process of entropy reduction is then suspended, as if it had neither beginning nor end, in a sort of sublimation of the third principle, creating a sense of timeless well-being. Indeed, the reduction of entropy is a source of well-being if it is continuous, but without meditation, anxiety reappears as soon as the entropic flow ceases.

Similarly, the "middle way" taught by Buddha uses information to navigate between mortification and indulgence. Because the flow of maximum energy passes through the middle, balance becomes the most efficient and sustainable state, avoiding dead ends and energy-draining extremes.

Entropy in Action

Let's return to our container of gas molecules. Initially, the observer could predict that the molecules would move from the hot side of the partition to the cold side because the observer had information about the experiment.

As mixing occurs, the ability of the observer to accurately predict what's occurring becomes less and less probable, until the movements of the molecules become unpredictable. At that point, maximum entropy is reached, which means a complete lack of information about the movements of these molecules. Entropy characterizes the microscopic disorder of a system, its degree of disorganization. It accounts for the degree of dispersion of energy (thermal, chemical, etc.)

within the system. According to the second law of thermodynamics, the energy of an isolated system tends to disperse as much as possible without any energy exchange with the outside.

Heat represents a degraded form of energy because its dissipation leads to a loss of free energy. Entropy is a measure of this degradation or dissipation of energy. When entropy increases, it corresponds to a reduction in free energy. The term "entropy" is a neologism introduced in 1865 by physicist Rudolf Clausius to succinctly formulate the second law of thermodynamics, which states that the entropy of an isolated system (receives no energy) can only increase. Energy must be supplied to a system to reduce its entropy. In the International System of Units, entropy is measured in joules per kelvin (J/K).

Entropy: From Theory to Practice

At absolute zero temperature, entropy reaches zero: everything achieves perfect order, and all motion ceases in a state of thermodynamic death. Consider a refrigerator: it uses electrical energy for two purposes. First, it reduces internal entropy by cooling (slowing the motion of air molecules inside), and second, it transfers the resulting heat to the surrounding air.

Another example illustrating this concept appears in flat-pack furniture assembly. The entropy associated with a new flat-pack decreases when we read the assembly instructions. Without instructions, however, the entropy increases dramatically. We can no longer easily evaluate (predict) the effort required for assembly.

Entropy is a quantity relative to the observer. Depending on my experience, assembling the furniture will take more or less time. In general, the transmission of information, which equates to a reduction in entropy, is neither perfect nor instantaneous from one observer to another.

This precise definition places entropy within both time and space while emphasizing its relativity. Even more abstract than energy itself, entropy measures an observer's uncertainty about how a system will evolve. For the average person, it refers to the uncertainty about the changes in their environment. Depending on their level of aversion to uncertainty, an individual will experience entropic stress, which resembles anxiety. A person with a Yin tendency seeks to blend into their environment and will feel it more intensely than a person with a Yang tendency, who is more focused on conquering their environment. I remember a remark my son made when he was nine years old: "When Mom packs her suitcase, she fills 60% of it with just-in-case." A perceptive observation that I've found true with all the women I've traveled with. For many, uncertainty rhymes with anxiety.

A low level of entropy is often associated with a state of serenity and confidence in the future. Consequently, the reduction of entropy is directly linked to well-being. Anxiety generally stems from difficulty in processing the information needed to reduce this entropy. An anxious person often feels an inability to maximize the energy flow they are supposed to transform. For example, a narcissistic manager who projects their unpredictable nature onto their team's work environment only increases the team's entropy – that is, their discomfort. The members of this team will want to leave to reduce their entropy and join another leader who provides clear direction and rules.

Psychopaths, dictators, and narcissistic manipulators amplify disorder within a system by fostering unpredictability, increasing entropy, and thereby draining energy from those affected. The difficulty of distinguishing right from wrong can also be understood through the lens of entropy. Like entropy, the perception of evil depends on the observer. Doing good or evil affects the observer's entropy.

Low entropy reflects a stable environment or one with a predictable evolution. Maximum entropy corresponds to a uniform distribution where all possible future states have the same probability. If a craftsman's workshop contains *n* tools and each tool has two possible states (stored or placed on the workbench), the workshop can take 2^n possible states.

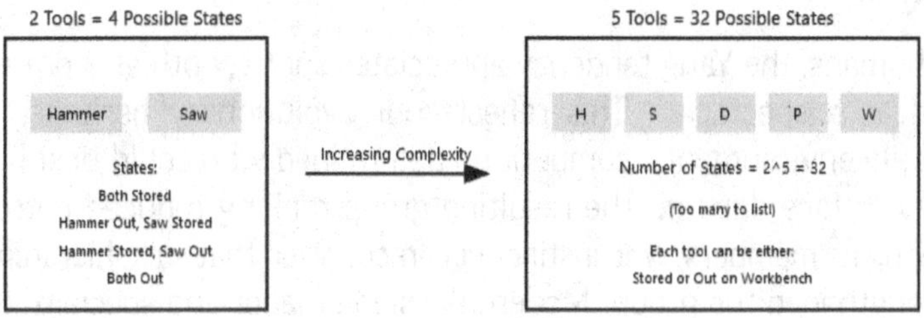

From this simple observation emerges a primary, obvious point: as a system grows more complex, acquiring a wider range of possible future states with non-negligible probability, the probability of any particular state occurring decreases. The evolution of a complex system is, therefore, largely unpredictable.

Consider a porcelain shop manager observing his domain. His entropy remains low when expecting calm, polite customers. A security guard at the entrance reduces entropy further. But should an agitated elephant approach the shop, entropy spikes dramatically. The manager's reduced entropy manifests physically as increased flow through his shop.

Darwinian evolution demonstrates the correspondence between maximizing energy flow and minimizing entropy, particularly in the distinction between carnivorous (Yang) and herbivorous (Yin) mammals. Carnivores capture a significantly higher energy flow through their diet and reduce their entropy through the evolution of their morphology, which pushes them to the top of the food chain. Herbivores, on the other hand, access a lower energy flow linked to plant growth, which limits their negentropic capacity.[4] They face greater uncertainty due to the presence of predators in their environment.

Maximizing our well-being involves reducing our perceived entropy, thereby maximizing the energy flow we can capture. Let's see how this simple observation applies to daily life and explains our behaviors.

Sports

In humans, the Yang tendency appreciates sports, both as a practice and as a spectacle. This reflects our evolutionary heritage. In hostile environments, competition determined who could best hunt prey or face danger. The resulting group ranking reduced entropy among its members, who instinctively recognized that such hierarchies strengthened the group. Modern division of labor and specialization within human society follow the same logic.

Countryside

The rapid alteration of a natural landscape, such as the installation of wind turbines, causes discomfort because it leads to an increase in the observer's entropy. Their living environment, the most visible part of their surroundings that they believed to be unchanging, becomes unpredictable. The anxiety - inducing effect of entropy is heightened when this change comes from decision - makers whom the observer does not know, leaving the observers with no clear path to reduce their entropy.

Education

Performance evaluations, like sports competitions, reduce entropy for Yang learners and enhance their well - being. Conversely, the Yin learner may perceive evaluation as a challenge to their connections with others, creating a sense of an informal hierarchy. Connecting with others remains the preferred method for the Yin to adapt to their environment and reduce their entropy. Therefore, Yang is more inclined toward meritocracy, while Yin leans towards egalitarianism.

Information & Energy

When you navigate unfamiliar terrain using GPS, you reduce your level of entropy relative to your goal. In other words, the information provided by the GPS is equivalent to energy. This equivalence can be quantified – if a journey takes two hours with GPS versus three hours without, the GPS information equals the energy saved from that hour of avoided walking.

In a given context, information represents energy saved, which can then be used for other purposes. This establishes a fundamental connection between information and energy, similar to the mass-energy relationship. It represents an equivalence rather than equality. Although we measure entropy in joules per kelvin, mass in grams, and energy in joules, they remain intrinsically linked.

The variation in entropy, noting that information allows for a reduction in entropy (negentropy), can thus be interpreted as the variation in the energy used by a system to transition from one state to another. Unlike mass, however, information received ages and can eventually become obsolete as systems evolve and possible states change over time. Mass-energy, by contrast, remains constant. The higher the entropy of a system, the more information is required to specify its microscopic state. The dissipation of energy—an increase in entropy for an observer outside the system— represents a loss of information about the system. Any increase in entropy leads to a decrease in the ability to produce free energy. A living organism counters this tendency by storing information to reduce its entropy, allowing it to capture more energy that it converts into mechanical work.

Scientific research progressively reduces societal entropy, enabling increased production of free energy—energy that converts to work before eventual heat dissipation. Entropy appears as both a property of the observer and of the observed system. In effect, information replicates but does not propagate instantaneously or evenly, as not all observers possess the same level of information. The relativity of entropy concerning the observer is further supported by the fact that not all observers have the same cognitive abilities. Some minds readily connect patterns that others might miss entirely.

We have observed two distinct paths for maximizing energy capture: the Yin path of establishing more connections with one's environment (Yin, the essence of the feminine in Taoist philosophy) and the Yang path of direct energy source control (Yang, the essence of the masculine).

Information & Beliefs

Environmental connections enhance predictability, thereby reducing entropy. When I am part of a group, I have a better ability to anticipate the decisions made by that group than if I were an outsider. In his book *Sapiens*, Yuval Harari explains how human groups form around shared beliefs, which serve as a means of reducing Yin entropy.

While beliefs reduce entropy within the group, machines offer an even more reliable entropy reduction. You can be more certain of the work it will produce than if you were to rely on people for the same task. The machine's needs, such as its energy supply and maintenance, are more predictable than human behavior. Therefore, the design and construction of the machine reduce the entropy of "Yang."

To build its machine, Yang uses knowledge and scientific proof rather than relying on belief. Belief is Yin, proof is Yang. Yin and Yang represent two ends of a spectrum rather than binary opposites, just as belief and proof are connected by the winding path of truth. A belief sometimes contains an aspect of truth, while proof often requires a degree of faith in scientific discoveries. In practice, using or relying on knowledge does not require one to replicate all physical experiments or demonstrate all the mathematical theorems that underpin them.

Neuroscientists have identified a synaptic receptor named NMDA, which might play a crucial role in our adherence to beliefs. When substances like ketamine block this receptor, the feeling of uncertainty in complex situations is heightened, leading to a weakening of critical thinking about new information. Confirmation bias only amplifies this tendency.

Believers prioritize the comfort of belief over the satisfaction of verification. It is estimated that 85% of the world's population holds some form of belief.[5] Yet, a mind opened by the wonder of science serves us better than one closed by the certainties of belief. Wonder and its corollary gratitude arise from a deep connection with reality. Shared beliefs can mobilize a large group to achieve certain goals, but if what unites them is based on a lie, the consequences can be devastating. Take, for example, intensive rhinoceros poaching. The horn, made merely of keratin – a protein found in our hair and nails –

gains perceived value solely through belief in nonexistent medicinal properties.

Too Much Information?

Mindfulness offers a different approach to information processing – immersing ourselves in our environment without judgment, rather than continuous analytical processing. The practice of mindfulness allows us to sift through and discard irrelevant information, in essence, what does not interest us.

Order is a way of storing and exchanging information, much like a computer, which makes information usable. Similarly, energy must be made usable in the process of wealth creation. Since information is equivalent to energy, creating order corresponds to creating wealth. This explains the success of companies engaged in systematically capturing private data, particularly – but not exclusively – the GAFAM (Google, Apple, Facebook, Amazon, and Microsoft) companies.

In living beings, sleep represents an alternation in the capture of information, allowing information to be sorted and stored in memory. This makes sleep an essential phase for entropy reduction.

6. Information

Information is data that allows the release or conservation of a certain amount of energy. The entropy of the observed system measures the lack of information about that system.

Before illustrating this definition with examples, it is important to briefly recall some theoretical concepts.

First, equivalence does not mean equality. In the famous equation $E = mc^2$, there is a proportionality factor, namely the speed of light squared.

Therefore, one can say that a mass is equivalent to energy, but a mass will never be equal to energy. Similarly, Boltzmann's equation $S = k \log W$ relates entropy S to energy W, expressed in J/K, which is the amount of energy required to change the temperature of a system by one degree. The factor here is k, Boltzmann's constant.

The second principle suggests another equivalence – between energy and entropy – indicating that energy is necessary to change the entropy of an isolated system. However, entropy is equivalent to information, as information is precisely defined as data that allows the entropy of a system to vary.

Thus, information is equivalent to a quantity of energy, just as an object with mass is.

For example, let's consider Bob, a tourist walking around Paris who wants to get to the Louvre on foot from his hotel located north of the city. Without receiving any electronic information, he wanders around, gets lost, asks for directions, and finally reaches the Louvre after an hour and a half of walking. His twin brother Charles, who set out at the same time and used a GPS, reaches the destination in one hour. We can conclude that the data received by Charles constitutes information equivalent to the energy of half an hour of walking, which is the energy Charles saved thanks to the information provided by the GPS.

False information corresponds to negative energy because it leads to energy waste rather than energy conservation. We gather information through attention, a process requiring brain power, which represents energy flow expressed in joules per second. Therefore, attention multiplied by time corresponds to energy.

We use this energy to reduce our entropy, that is, our uncertainty about the evolution of our environment. In other words, when something captures our attention, it captures a portion of our energy. Capturing our information, as Facebook or other social networks might do, effectively harvests the energy we have spent gathering data to reduce our entropy. These networks become the creators and editors of our digital identities.

Social networks primarily capture our behavioral and intentional data. Another highly valuable type of information is digital money, created, stored, and managed by banks. Digital currency is information that represents our labor as information, while credit money goes even further. It monetizes future energy, the energy we must provide to repay.

Since an amount of money represents an amount of energy, we can say that data capture translates into a quasi-monetary capture. This explains why GAFAM companies accumulate phenomenal wealth at a rate only comparable to banks. Just like energy, information can exist as a stock (such as books or a reputation) or as a flow (like news agencies or news channels), depending on whether it evolves sporadically (as in successive editions of a book) or continuously.

Consider how different information types release varying amounts of energy. For example, a stream of sports information provides well-being that releases a small amount of energy in the recipient. A fan is re-energized when their team wins. They feel closer to the victors, who, through the display of their strength, offer a fleeting sense of security. This contrasts sharply with GPS information, which saves hikers substantial physical energy. As the energetic utility of information decreases, it approaches entertainment, which only temporarily reduces the entropy of its audience. When utility becomes null, the information is merely data. The energetic criterion allows us to assess the degree of utility of data, determining whether it constitutes true information.

The philosopher Pascal anticipated this fundamental distinction through his principle of inquietude, differentiating between the distracted self, who receives an unexpected flow of information, and the anxious subject, who seeks to reduce their entropy. However, without the concepts of energy and entropy, Pascal's insights, though prescient, remained bound within the realm of magical thinking.

According to Austrian economist Ludwig von Mises (1881-1973), the major challenge in economics lies in the coordination of multiple agents, each possessing imperfect, tacit, and often subjective information. The goal is to collectively optimize the use of available resources to produce goods and services that meet the needs of society.

Societal complexity grows in lockstep with information volume. Profit serves as the fundamental incentive driving this coordination, rewarding the success of an enterprise. At the heart of this mechanism is the price formation process. The prices of goods and services represent the crucial information that allows economic agents to exchange value on a consensual basis. This insight underpins game theory, a branch of mathematics that studies economic incentives among different agents. The centrally planned economy of the USSR quickly declined soon after a central bureaucracy took control of pricing. It could survive as long as 70 years only by exploiting its enormous oil and gas resources.

Imagine that tomorrow, artificial intelligence (AI) will replace the invisible hand of the market to determine prices. Such an AI system would require access to high-quality data – data that only emerges from efficient market operations. If the economy becomes too centralized and profits are mainly captured by a central authority, the incentives to act by producing and using quality data disappear. The result? Arbitrary price distortions and a decline in data quality.

"Freedom of opinion is a farce if information on the facts is not guaranteed."

– Hannah Arendt

7. Time

If energy is imperishable and uncreated, and time is infinite, then energy must inevitably pass through all possible states an infinite number of times. This principle opens intriguing possibilities about the nature of existence itself.

If time is infinite, it may not be necessary to search for extraterrestrial life in space but rather in time. Indeed, if chance has an infinite amount of time ahead of it, the recurrence of an event like the emergence of the human species becomes infinitely probable. Our cognitive bias leads us to imagine this occurrence within our own lifetime rather than in a temporal beyond. Therefore, one might believe in reincarnation because every living being, every thing, is a form of energy that could reappear identically in an infinite future, with an infinitesimal but non-zero probability.

For the same reason, games like chess were discovered, not invented, as they could have already existed before the first game was ever played. Since time has no beginning, one could indeed find an occurrence of the game of chess in an infinitely distant past. As the German mathematician David Hilbert explained when addressing philosopher Auguste Comte's failure to find an unsolvable problem, such problems simply do not exist. His motto, "We must know, we will know," implicitly acknowledges infinite time. The explanation of any phenomenon pre-exists in the universe of possibilities simply because the phenomenon is observed.

Previously, Ludwig Colding's work described the "forces of nature" as imperishable and uncreated, implicitly leading to viewing time as a dimension without beginning or end. Modern cosmology supports that the Big Bang is just a phase of contraction followed by a sudden expansion in an infinite series of fluctuations, characteristic of dissipative structures.

It is also widely accepted that entropy introduces the notion of the arrow of time. Unlike the three dimensions of space in which we live, time cannot be traversed backward. This fundamental asymmetry manifests in everyday experiences. It is easy to squeeze toothpaste out of its tube but very difficult to put it back in. Similarly, it is easy to mix coffee and milk but difficult to separate them once mixed. The entropy of the coffee with milk is greater than the entropy of the milk and coffee measured separately. This difference, called the entropy of mixing, can only be reduced by supplying energy to separate them again. Since the power required for this task is not infinite, it requires a certain amount of time. The mixing process is, therefore, not reversible because separation after mixing would take much longer, whereas mixing happens almost instantly.

Every energy transformation is practically imperfect and is accompanied by an increase in entropy, making it partially irreversible. This introduces the perception of time's flow on a macroscopic scale.

Life itself represents a journey through different energy states. If our life experience is the traversal of different states of energy, the second law of thermodynamics indicates that we travel through these states on one-way paths. We cannot turn back, and returning to a previous state requires a significant detour. This principle is consistent with our status as dissipative structures. We can capture energy, but we cannot reverse the direction of the energy flow that passes through us.

Yet, interestingly, over a very short time interval (less than a billionth of a second), in certain quantum physics experiments involving photons, it is impossible to determine which event occurs before the other. It seems that the concept of time briefly disappears for the observed photons.

There are at least two other distortions of time: the perception of time depending on age and the passage of time relative to speed.

According to the law of diminishing returns, for the same amount of energy used, the relative decrease in entropy slows with age, which explains the impression that time passes more quickly in adulthood than when we were children. In childhood, everything is new, and therefore, almost all the data we receive constitutes information—data that steadily reduces our uncertainty about our environment. This happiness experienced in childhood inevitably diminishes with age.

This also explains why we feel that time flows differently when we are in a new environment (such as on vacation in the tropics or the mountains), where fresh information floods our senses. In such situations, we feel invigorated because our capacity to process the energy flow that passes through us suddenly increases. We need to gather information to reduce our entropy. Upon returning, we may feel that the vacation week lasted two or three times longer than it actually did, simply because a lot of new information was received and is being organized in our memory. This information brings about the sense of well-being that accompanies any reduction in entropy and is what vacationers seek when traveling to distant lands.

The second law of thermodynamics dictates that the entropy of a closed system increases over time. More precisely, an isolated system, thrown out of equilibrium, will spontaneously evolve towards maximum entropy. When faced with a closed system, the observer can thus perceive the passage of time through the continuous and spontaneous increase in entropy. The passage of time and its measurement provide information that reduces the observer's own entropy.

The second law bestows time with its arrow – the level of entropy in a closed system must increase until it reaches an equilibrium state where entropy is maximal. This principle offers a temporal compass. By measuring entropy at two points, we can determine their chronological order with certainty. For instance, if we observe a photo of Rudolf Clausius illustrating the second law, we can say with certainty that this photo was taken before his death.

The evolution of dissipative structures, as described by the third law, characterized by cycles of expansion and contraction or birth and death, also contributes to our perception of the passage of time. These universal pulses mark time's passage at every scale of existence.

In *The End of Certainties* (1996), Ilya Prigogine challenged the notion that time's arrow merely reflects our imperfect knowledge:

> *Irreversibility can no longer be attributed to a mere appearance that would disappear if we attained perfect knowledge. It is an essential condition for the coherent behavior of billions upon billions of molecules. As I like to repeat, matter is blind to equilibrium where the arrow of time does not manifest; but when it does, far from equilibrium, matter begins to see! Without the coherence of irreversible non-equilibrium processes, the emergence of life on Earth would be inconceivable. The thesis that the arrow of time is only phenomenological is absurd. It is not we who generate the arrow of time. On the contrary, we are its children.*

Time flows at the pace of entropy change. Our perception of time is relative because it depends on the rate at which our entropy changes. During a one-week trip to explore a distant country where everything is new to us, our entropy decreases more rapidly than usual, and our perception of time is consequently altered.

It is as if an acceleration in the decrease of entropy slows down our perception of time. This explains why a year in our youth seems much longer than a year in middle age, as if time speeds up as we grow older. The accumulation of knowledge and experience reduces our entropy but slows our entropic flow, as indicated by the law of diminishing returns. Over time, our exposure to new knowledge and discoveries progressively diminishes.

These everyday experiences of time mirror Einstein's relativity. For example, an astronaut traveling at a speed close to that of light would age more slowly than those who remained on Earth. In summary, the less change or movement, the faster time seems to pass. The decrease in our entropy is a decreasing function of our speed through time.

Mathematician Ricardo Perez-Marco locates time's perception in our neural architecture, specifically the decentralized structure of neurons. Our brain assigns no master controller to time. No single area of the brain or specific category of neurons controls time, implying that neurons function as a decentralized network of timekeepers. While certain areas may be specialized, these specializations are not hierarchically organized, nor do they culminate in a master area that dominates the others. Consequently, in the absence of a conductor, neurons synchronize in waves, much like the validators of the Bitcoin network synchronize at average intervals of 10 minutes. The frequency of neural waves is, in fact, of the same order of magnitude as the smallest time interval we can perceive.

Synchronization periods are an optimization tradeoff. Shorter intervals allow more frequent network connections, but neurons must balance communication with computation. Just as an artist would struggle to create if they had to talk to their audience constantly rather than having quiet periods punctuated by conversations or presentations, excessive communication overwhelms neurons and paralyzes their actual information processing.

The synchronization period of neurons, therefore, may shape our perception of time. This hypothesis is supported by the fact that this perception is disrupted or even disappears during sleep or unconsciousness, when the frequency of neural synchronization waves changes.

This phenomenon of spontaneous synchronization within a decentralized network is not unique to neurons but can be observed throughout nature, perhaps most magically in fireflies. Each firefly has an internal clock that causes it to emit a light signal at more or less regular intervals. Instead of synchronizing with the help of a central conductor, each firefly follows a remarkably simple adjustment algorithm. As night falls, it starts slowly, but when it sees the light of a nearby firefly, it slightly speeds up its own rhythm. As demonstrated by Nicky Case with his simulation[6], this simple adjustment is enough to quickly synchronize an entire swarm of fireflies across kilometers!

More generally, the phenomenon of emergence, a seemingly spontaneous synchronization, occurs when a multitude of actors (neurons, bacteria, swarms of insects or birds, crowds of humans, etc.) adopt predictable behavior based on immediate individual decisions. Turn left or turn right? Attack or retreat? Buy or sell? These simple and immediate decisions fall under what psychologist and economist Daniel Kahneman calls "fast thinking," the quick, emotionally driven reflexes that contrast with more deliberate, thoughtful decision-making.

Ultimately, our perception of time is intimately linked to complexity. A water molecule does not ponder whether it can reverse time because its lifespan is infinitely longer compared to ours. A configuration that occurred in the past has an extremely low but non-zero probability of recurring. Over an infinite span of time, the probability becomes a certainty: the particle will inevitably re-enter a past configuration at some point in the future. Energy, therefore, has no sense of time, and the fact that it is condensed into the form of a living organism merely represents an occurrence of an event that will recur an infinite number of times.

Our brains did not evolve to easily manipulate the concept of infinity because, unlike the concept of passing time, it has no immediate practical applications for humans. On the contrary, the evolution of the species necessitates a cycle of births, which induces the perception of passing time. Evolution thus prompts the two effects of the third law: self-organization through long-term natural selection and the motivation of each individual to maximize the flow of energy captured in the short term.

The same evolutionary constraints that shaped our perception of time also limit our ability to conceptualize infinitesimally short time intervals or near-light speeds. Thus, the famous dialogue between Bergson and Einstein revealed the philosopher's errors, as he did not grasp the physicist's mathematical language or scientific reasoning.

Their discussion mainly focused on the philosophical implications of special relativity, particularly through the "twin paradox" (originally conceived by the French physicist Paul Langevin, a contemporary of Einstein). This thought experiment compares two clocks: one remains on Earth, while the other embarks on a round-trip journey into space. By comparing the readings of the two clocks upon departure and return, one should be able to verify that time dilates (i.e., passes more slowly) at high speeds. In practice, however, this experiment is difficult to carry out because the speed of a rocket is far below the speed of light. Even so, evidence of time dilation is observable through particle accelerators or cosmic rays.

8. Principles

A physical principle is a rule that explains and measures physical phenomena, with varying degrees of precision depending on experimental conditions. Just as the application of law in practice falls to the discretion of a judge, who in the realm of criminal law adheres to the principle of individualizing punishment, the application of a physical principle depends on its context.

For example, the principle of conservation of mass applies in classical mechanics at normal speeds but breaks down in special relativity when speeds approach that of light. The universe is defined as the largest dissipative structure we can observe. Georges Lemaître (1894–1966), a Catholic priest and Belgian physicist, discovered that the universe was expanding before Edwin Hubble confirmed it with a giant telescope in 1929. Lemaître proposed that the Big Bang resulted from the explosion of a primordial atom, whose expansion continues to this day. He was convinced that physical laws are not universal but apply to subsets of the universe. If space and time are infinite, this implies an infinity of parallel universes and an infinity of laws, possibly contradictory, that could be simultaneously at work somewhere. This elegant idea addresses those skeptics who believe that only a few simple physical principles are sufficient to describe our universe.

This brings us to Taoism (in Chinese, "teaching of the way"), one of the main philosophical currents in Chinese thought alongside Confucianism and Buddhism. Taoism posits the existence of a principle at the origin of all things, called "Tao," in a way that anticipates thermodynamics. I consider this a coincidence, but mystics might interpret the three principles of thermodynamics as a manifestation of the Tao, as they both deal with the flows of energy between polarized energy stocks.

In Taoism, Yin and Yang are two forms of energy with opposing polarities, establishing a framework for interpreting natural phenomena as flows of energy. We can apply this Taoist symbolism of Yin and Yang in an anthropological approach that distinguishes opposing and complementary behavioral tendencies in human societies. These symbols, like mathematical symbols, help structure thought around abstract concepts, but their use does not imply a regression to magical thinking. Rather, they provide a useful lens for understanding complex dynamics in both nature and society.

Part 2: Economy and Currency

9. Bitcoin

Bitcoin is the first decentralized network established through a computer protocol. Designed by Satoshi Nakamoto, the protocol was published on October 31, 2008, and has powered the Bitcoin network since its inception.

What makes Bitcoin unique is its operation without a central authority, resembling an *anarchic* system that aims to establish a social order without a dominant power. Many mistakenly equate anarchy with chaos, but this association tends to discredit this decentralized political system in favor of a vertical, centralized power. Switzerland is a working example of ordered anarchy: a limited federal power balanced by the cantons' authority so that no one truly knows who governs. The Swiss political system, resulting in order without power, embodies the very definition of anarchy.

Bitcoin is money with or without the bank. Unlike politics, which creates dilemmas, Bitcoin creates new options. By identifying the monetary system as the main structuring element of society, preceding any political system, Bitcoin can be described as a radical solution, in the etymological sense of the term; it tackles the root of a problem. Radicalism is not synonymous with obsession or extremism, and those who do not recognize a primary cause are quick to accuse those who have identified one.

The system's sophisticated design rests on three theoretical pillars: 1) game theory (mathematics - incentive economics), 2) information theory (physics - thermodynamics), and 3) number theory (mathematics - cryptography). Game theory studies and models the incentives that shape behavior in the economy, that is, the exchanges of energy between rational agents. In contrast, communism is a system that ignores incentives and favors a planned economy. Economic incentives matter because they compensate for the risks and efforts inherent in entrepreneurship.

Without the freedom and incentive to undertake ventures, the decision to serve one need over another becomes the prerogative of the state and, ultimately, a bureaucratic administration. Price formation, the meeting point of supply and demand, is information that allows goods and services to be positioned on the common energy scale that a monetary system constitutes.

Remove price formation, notably the decision of which product should be manufactured, from the economic process, and you're left with central planning setting prices. Consequently, shortages or surpluses are often observed, linked to prices disconnected from reality, preventing a spontaneous and efficient meeting of supply and demand. Some ideologies, like communism, claim to transcend incentive mechanisms by replacing them with egalitarian motivations applied to everyone, everywhere. This totalitarianism has had the success, or lack thereof, with which we are familiar, for example, in the USSR, North Korea, Cambodia, and Venezuela.

Ideologues have a problem with Bitcoin. It has a tangible and real connection to energy through its proof-of-work. Although capitalism has undeniable problems, these stem not from the system itself but from the direct consequences of distortions created by unchecked monetary creation. In the absence of currency competition, capitalism transforms. Subsidized by monopolistic monetary creation directed towards an oligarchy, pure capitalism quickly degenerates into crony capitalism and predation.

The monopoly of state-issued currencies, what we might call "promise money," has two major consequences that mirror each other: the expansion of the welfare state and growing inequality. The welfare state grows because public authorities gain the ability to finance ever-expanding social aid programs. Meanwhile, banks finance electoral campaigns, foreshadowing the funding needs of political programs and their clientele.

This distorted system creates a two-tier society, with easy access to credit for some and impossible barriers for others, leading to an increase in wealth inequality. Favoring large enterprises over small ones exacerbates the concentration of capital. By changing the rules of monetary creation and especially by making them beyond the reach of regulatory capture, Bitcoin represents a true paradigm shift in monetary policy. Its adoption alongside state currencies, as seen in El Salvador, the first country to recognize it as legal tender in September 2021, offers the prospect of a possible balance between the monetization of the future through debt (state currency) and the anchoring of currency in present reality through energy (Bitcoin).

Bitcoin thus paves the way for a more rational form of capitalism, one protected from the distortions caused by unlimited monetary creation. Launched in 1991, Linux serves as a model for the adoption of open-source solutions (with publicly available code) like Bitcoin. Thanks to Linux, Microsoft's once-unshakable dominance through its proprietary Windows system began to erode. What once seemed unassailable proved vulnerable to open-source innovation. The competition between operating systems improved the resilience of the Web, enhanced digital sovereignty, and reduced software costs.

The globalization wave that began in the 1990s pushed countries toward specialized production, creating centralized hubs for production of each good and service. We're now seeing a counter-movement favoring local sovereignty and decentralization's inherent resilience, even at the cost of some efficiency. *Freedom has no price, but it has a cost.* Decentralization reflects this.

As fossil fuel supplies dwindle and affect prices, labor costs must decrease. For this, the labor supply must increase, either through the multiplication of machines (increased automation) or through mass immigration. Currently, only nuclear energy (fission today and fusion in the future, when perfected) can offset depleting fossil energy without further harming the climate and, above all, without requiring a radical and improbable change in behavior (energy capture, birth rates), as it would go against the third principle of thermodynamics.

Unfortunately, politicians often exploit these strategic issues – immigration, automation, and the environment –by manipulating emotions. In the monetary domain, the fear of change, perpetuated by the absolute control of monetary power exercised by central banks, stifles any debate on the consequences and costs of this monopoly. The Bitcoin protocol, on the other hand, encourages miners (network validators) to use the cheapest electricity possible, primarily from surplus production that no one else wants.

This is why the proof-of-work must involve a calculation that serves no purpose other than securing the Bitcoin network. Critics who do not grasp this fundamental point often lament that the calculation is not applied to something they consider useful, such as computing large prime numbers that cryptographers could use.

Indeed, if the computation could generate direct revenue instead of only the indirect revenue related to Bitcoin's security, miners might compete with other industrial uses of electricity. This would partially diminish Bitcoin mining's environmental benefit, which is its reliance on surplus energy or energy that would otherwise go to waste.

Currently, only distortions in the energy market, such as access to subsidized fossil fuels, would justify some miners using anything other than surplus energy. The value of this surplus collection lies in the signal it sends to industries using electrical energy. When Bitcoin miners set up operations somewhere, they signal the presence of surplus electricity.

An equilibrium can thus be found between currency production and the manufacturing of goods or services. Here's how: Globalization began in the 1970s as a way to find cheaper labor to offset the rising cost of oil. As human labor is increasingly replaced by robots, industrial production today is intrinsically linked to electricity production. Since electricity is more difficult to transport than automated production facilities, it is the factories that move closer to power plants.

By selling a portion of their electricity to Bitcoin miners, power producers signal to industrial companies that they can supply cheap electricity, and it won't be long before these companies take over from the miners. Miners who install their equipment in containers can quickly move to regions where industrial demand has not yet emerged. This process can then repeat itself for the next power plant experiencing a surplus of renewable energy.

German economist Guido Hülsmann explains the trade-off between industrial production and the mining of a commodity-currency: "As in any industry, currency-miners will be able to invest and increase their production capacity if and only if their return on investment is at least equal to what they could have achieved in other fields or industries."

Nuclear fusion could significantly alter the landscape by producing abundant surpluses. This could either devalue the cost of minting bitcoins or increase the difficulty of mining. Bitcoin would be affected, but likely no more than any other sector of the economy, for which this prospect of overabundant energy is dizzying.

Fusion will reach profitability when the famous ignition threshold is achieved, meaning when the energy released by hydrogen atoms (as in a star) exceeds the activation energy provided to them (by lasers or magnetic confinement).

This raises an interesting question: Is the industrial utility, like that of a commodity or raw material, an advantage or a disadvantage for a monetary system?

Consider water. Water has such significant industrial utility that it makes it unsuitable for use as currency. Bottling water and transporting it from a river (where it is abundant) to a desert significantly increases its value and amounts to wealth creation. But, a currency is expected to be easily and instantly transferable and to maintain roughly the same value across different locations.

Ideally, to avoid disruptions in price formation, the supply of money should not be impacted by non-monetary demand. Gold has industrial utility, like most metals, but its relative scarcity ensures that its supply remains inelastic in the face of a rise in demand that might be driven by this utility.

Bitcoin is even better equipped to address the issue of non-monetary utility, thanks to its limited and fixed supply. Even if demand increases, the issuance supply rate remains inelastic due to periodic difficulty adjustments every 2016 blocks, which help keep production capped at a predefined maximum level.

Bitcoin and Energy

The Bitcoin protocol incentivizes miners to engage in a continuous geographic arbitrage to obtain the cheapest electricity. Due to imperfections in the electricity market, in most cases, the cheapest electricity comes from production surpluses.

Unlike renewable energies, stock-based energies like uranium or fossil fuels are considered "dispatchable," meaning they don't generate surpluses. When demand decreases, it is always possible to reduce production by conserving the stock rather than burning it at a loss or with reduced profitability.

Renewable energies, on the other hand, are intermittent and cannot continuously adjust to fluctuating demand. Since electricity is difficult to store or transport over long distances, specific surpluses are associated with renewables. Bitcoin miners tap into this surplus, creating value from what would otherwise be wasted energy.

To put this in perspective, global electricity production exceeded 27,000 TWh per year in 2021, Bitcoin uses approximately 140 TWh. In other words, if electricity production generated only a 1% surplus, which is a very conservative estimate, Bitcoin would currently only monetize half of that surplus. This suggests significant room for growth without competing with essential power needs.

Bitcoin and the Dollar

If we compare the debt capacities globally, we notice that the United States enjoys a privileged position because the dollar serves as the reserve currency used by many central banks worldwide, allowing it to incur more debt than other advanced countries. The European Union, on the other hand, has never succeeded in establishing the euro as an international reserve currency.

"Dedollarizing" through Bitcoin, as El Salvador did by adopting Bitcoin as legal tender alongside the US dollar, is an option that Europe could consider to regain its sovereignty. However, this would require political parties to finally acknowledge monetary sovereignty as a key political issue. Without this recognition, Europe will become increasingly economically, technologically, and militarily subjugated by the United States.

Bitcoin and History

If history is written by the victors, central bankers aspire to influence the history of money. In 2014, I was invited to give a presentation on Bitcoin at the Journées de l'économie (Jéco), where I had the opportunity to explain the essentials in 30 minutes so that the audience could get a sense of this invention. However, the organizers deemed it necessary to split the speaking time with a historian from the American Federal Reserve (Fed)! Yes, you read that correctly. Central banks, with their unlimited means of monetary creation, pay historians to write the history of money in their own way and make it known to the public.

Moreover, both Mises' regression theorem and Aristotle's definition of money have been challenged by the invention of Bitcoin. Let's see how Bitcoin dismantles the regression theorem first. Then, in the chapter on money, we will expose Aristotle's definition of money as an authority argument misused by central banks.

Mises uses a reasoning process known as backward induction, a more precise term than "regression," to explain how money gains value. Mises conjectured that if a seller accepts gold as payment at time *t*, it's because they observed at time *t-1* that other sellers accepted it as payment. Similarly, those who attributed purchasing power to gold at time *t-1* did so because they observed that at time *t-2*, gold had comparable purchasing power. By tracing this reasoning through a process of backward induction to the first use of gold as currency, Mises concluded that the initial acceptor must have recognized gold's non-monetary value first.

Ultimately, the regression theorem asserts that all money derives its value from its non-monetary use. Thus, gold is said to derive its value from its use in jewelry production on the grounds that the first person to accept it as a means of payment would have first observed its utility to jewelers.

Even though the generalization made by this conjecture (the term "Mises conjecture" would be more precise than "theorem") is questionable on its own, Bitcoin offers multiple industrial uses. It is indeed a global network, available 24/7 for payments, secure messaging, recording tamper-proof timestamps, and certifying data files. These applications emerged from the computing power developed to secure Bitcoin's monetary network.

Interestingly, Bitcoin does more than challenge Mises' assumption; it inverts it. It is the security required by a payment network, measured by the computing power of the miners, that makes the time-stamping and certification unalterable. In the case of Bitcoin, one could argue that the monetary system, and more specifically, the process of monetary creation, initially subsidizes its industrial uses. However, the network could eventually operate independently of this subsidy. It would then align with other peer-to-peer networks, like email, which function based on the services provided, monetized through subscriptions or advertising.

Intrinsic Value

Intrinsic value does not exist despite widespread belief to the contrary. The value attributed to a good or service is always subjective, depending on the preferences of each individual. To illustrate this, consider a house that has become uninhabitable due to age and must be demolished. It then has a negative value corresponding to the cost of demolition. Even the land on which it stands has no intrinsic value, and if it is polluted, its value could become zero or negative once the cost of cleanup is factored in. Value depends on the context and the observer; it is information, which equates to a variation in entropy, and entropy depends on the context and the observer.

Anyone who uses the argument of intrinsic value is, therefore, ignoring the second law of thermodynamics and the concept of entropy. Typically, those who invoke intrinsic value often do so to argue that something is worthless because they do not see its utility.

Bitcoin derives its value from its inherent properties, such as divisibility, transferability, verifiability, and scarcity. Like any value, it is not intrinsic, as it exists only for those who appreciate and value these properties.

Acquisition and Transaction Confirmation

Another frequently misunderstood concept is transaction speed. Processing time differs from acquisition time. The processing time of a monetary transaction is defined by the duration between the initiation of a payment and the moment when the received amount can be spent. In the case of an electronic payment, the acquisition by the network is almost instantaneous, regardless of whether via the Bitcoin network or a banking network. However, with a credit card payment, merchants might wait several days or even months for guaranteed access to the funds. For a payment made with Bitcoin, however, the merchant can spend the received amount after an average of ten minutes, once the transaction is recorded in the blockchain.

In summary, the acquisition of an electronic transaction by a network occurs within seconds, but the processing time of the transaction depends on the network, ranging from ten minutes for Bitcoin to several hours for a banking network. Thus, speed comparisons should focus on processing time, not acquisition time, which is nearly instantaneous for all electronic transactions.

10. Inflation

The common definition of inflation as "a generalized and continuous increase in the price level" misses the mark. This naive definition reflects the confusion perpetuated by bankers between the increase in the money supply and the rise in prices. In the context of monetary monopoly, these two phenomena overlap: bankers influence the first, and the public suffers the second as a consequence of the first.

If the money supply increases by 10% per year, it effectively quadruples over a period of ten years. Any good, service, or wage that does not keep pace with this increase is thus devalued by the same amount. When wages remain stable while real estate prices quadruple, workers face an increasingly burdensome and substantial cost of housing relative to their income.

To better understand this dynamic, we must first recognize that when we accept money as a monthly salary in exchange for our work, we are exchanging our labor for a representation of energy. The worker's labor is a flow of energy that, when integrated over a month, corresponds to the stock of energy delivered in the form of money by their employer. The currency must represent this amount of energy for the work-salary exchange to be balanced.

Money can exist in three different forms:

1. Commodity Currency (like gold) - A gold coin represents a certain stock of energy (a certain mass of gold: $E = mc^2$) and provides physical proof of the energy expended extracting the ore, minting the coin, and securing it until it is exchanged.

2. Energy-Backed Money (like Bitcoin) - Each fraction of Bitcoin contains mathematical proof of the energy used to mine and secure it until it is exchanged.

3. Energy-Promise Money (like euros or company shares) - Each monetary unit carries a promise of future energy provided by a counterparty. With euros, a borrower promises to provide energy through loan repayment. When banks issue loans, they create money; when borrowers repay, that money is destroyed. In practice, there are always more bank loans issued than repaid, so the amount of euros in circulation increases over time. With shares, the company will provide energy to shareholders in the form of future profits.

Energy-promise money, issued in exchange for the promise of debt repayment, is easy to create. Bankers are tempted to create more and more of it because the energy counterpart is provided by the borrower, not the banker. As a result, energy-promise money finances increasingly less useful projects, from the arms industry to oil extraction, at the risk of depleting resources and destroying our environment.

Oil shares the same fate as rhinoceros horns. Just as poachers will hunt the last rhinos to the point of extinction for their horns, oil companies will seek out the last drops of oil. The temptation to create money is even greater because monetary creation costs bankers nothing, allowing them to accumulate promises of repayment while collecting various fees and interest along the way. They can also discreetly allocate loans, preferably to those who already hold assets, increasing debtors' dependence on banks.

Most importantly, banks can acquire assets, either directly by lending to themselves or indirectly by lending to their obligors, before the prices of these assets rise due to monetary inflation. The gradual increase in prices slowly replaces the ownership of goods with mere usage to the benefit of the service provider. The rental model is expanding to almost all sectors.

The generation born after 1980, known as "millennials," is increasingly unable to own their homes, often condemned to pay rent until they inherit property, if they are fortunate. The inflation of real estate prices is directly linked to monetary creation through credit, which dilutes the value of money, and to the growing demand for housing driven by population growth, either through birth rates in emerging countries or immigration in developed countries.

This dynamic of rising prices extends to other goods, making them more accessible through renting rather than buying. The winners? The lenders who finance landlords and the landlords themselves are growing wealthier at the expense of other economic actors.

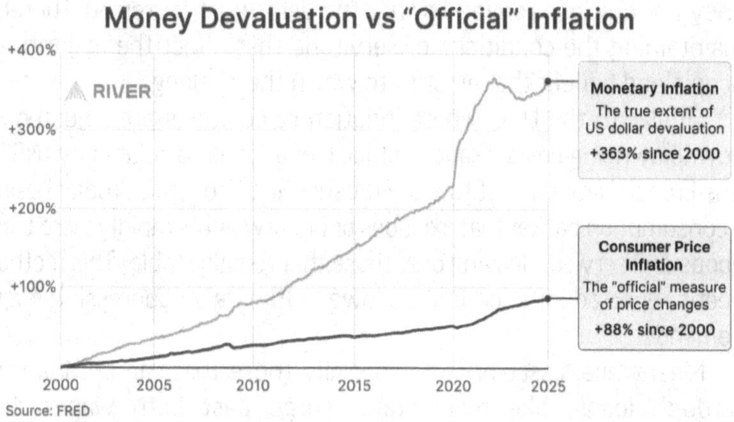

In a monetary monopoly, the inflation of the money supply results in rising prices of assets acquired by the first recipients of newly created money, a phenomenon described in 1730 by economist Richard Cantillon in his work *Essai sur la Nature du Commerce en Général*, known as the Cantillon Effect. Real estate and stock prices rise following money's entry points into the economic circuit, primarily through mortgage loans and loans to publicly traded companies.

This explains why salaries in New York's financial sector are very high; New York is the entry point for monetary creation by the U.S. central bank. Similarly, Frankfurt, home to the European Central Bank (ECB), is wealthier than Berlin, the political capital, a unique situation in Europe.

Price formation is distorted by the limitless creation of energy-promise money, similar to what happened in the USSR with central economic planning. To understand the extent to which the future energy of borrowers has been preempted by traditional finance, by early 2024, the global amount of energy-promise money stood at \$87,250 billion.[7] In comparison, the energy monetized by Bitcoin, the energy-proof currency, represented only \$1,000 billion.[8]

Orthodox defenders of the banking system do not hesitate to claim that "real" inflation is wage inflation. According to them, wage inflation is particularly dangerous because it could trigger an increase in interest rates by the central bank and, consequently, raise the cost of debt. They are quick to remind us that the debt must be repaid, thereby maintaining the conditions of servitude that affect the majority of people and benefit the minority to which they belong.

Similar to the U.S., where inflation calculations are adjusted to downplay rising costs, France's official inflation is calculated by INSEE (the French National Institute of Statistics and Economic Studies) using a consumption basket that excludes or underweights rapidly increasing goods and services, leaving only those that remain stable. This method keeps reported inflation figures lower, ultimately suppressing wage demands.

Meanwhile, asset prices, especially those that can be financed through loans, like real estate, surge past both wages and non-debt-financed service prices. This leads to an increase in the value of patrimonial assets measured in euros, while wages remain relatively stable, widening the wealth gap between wage earners and rentiers.

INSEE defends its opacity with a curious logic. As Jean-Louis L'héritier, head of the consumer prices, resources, and living conditions department at INSEE, stated: "To avoid any manipulation by actors involved in the economic circuit of product commercialization, it's clear that it's better to keep the products secret." The irony is rich. They suggest that other economic actors are less trustworthy than INSEE itself, which, serving the government, has every reason to minimize the inflation rate and does so freely.

As Mark Twain aptly summarized: "There are three kinds of lies: lies, damned lies, and statistics."

Another symptom of price inflation can be observed in the rise of stock markets. The increase in the CAC40 index does not necessarily reflect an increase in the value of companies, but rather an increase in the price of shares in euros, a currency diluted by monetary creation. Unfortunately, wages do not keep pace with this rise because not all companies benefit equally from monetary creation; bankers prioritize real estate development and large corporations.

Since energy-promise money monetizes the future energy of borrowers, there is a temptation to impose it through a monopoly to strengthen its grip on as many borrowers as possible and keep them indebted for as long as possible, especially through mortgage loans. This monopoly amplifies the flaws of debt-based money: it reduces the motivation to deliver quality service, erodes societal resilience by tying everything to a fragile, crisis-prone system, and subordinates political authority to a monetary power that ultimately controls public funding. The central bank's legally enshrined independence only reinforces this dominance over democratic institutions.

Electoral rules have eroded meaningful debate in favor of escalating false promises. This dynamic severely complicates the ecological transition. A sustainable economy would prioritize long-term projects, thus delaying the banker's reward compared to more lucrative short-term ventures like the fossil fuel industry.

The system maintains its grip through the mandated use of the euro, if only to pay wages and taxes, leaving us no choice but to participate. Even if an alternative were available, we would likely be tempted to spend the inflationary currency (the euro) first for purchases, wages, and taxes. If another currency is perceived as a better store of value, it would be hoarded rather than used as a medium of exchange, as per the adage that "bad money drives out good," known as Gresham's law.

Another harmful effect of the monetary monopoly is its legal and regulatory framework, which marginalizes alternative currencies, demonizing them in the eyes of the public and the media. It would be as illogical as banning charging stations on highways and then declaring electric cars useless. Yet, this is precisely what happens with decentralized payment networks. It's hardly necessary to ask who benefits from this absurd situation.

Inflation and Demography

Our understanding of energy shapes our vision of the world and the future. It is inseparable from our conception of money. Unlimited money leads to the depletion of natural resources: with promise money, all projects can be financed, including those detrimental to the planet. The monopoly of centralized promise money inevitably increases inequality.

An energy-based monetary standard like Bitcoin would provide a more accurate and fair measurement of economic exchanges, reflecting actual energy flows. It would also allow us to move away from the promise-money monopoly, whose justification grows more obscure as its disadvantages become more evident.

Unlimited money also accompanies the phenomenal inflation of the global population, often downplayed by experts appointed by demographic institutes. In 1800, the global population was one billion; by 1960, it was three billion; today, we are approaching eight billion. Current trends lead experts to predict that we will reach nearly 10 billion by 2050.

This explosive growth is unevenly distributed. In Africa, for example, the average birth rate is nearly four and a half children per woman, compared to one and a half children per woman in Europe. The population of Africa, including North Africa, is expected to triple by the end of the century, according to the UN, reaching over 4 billion.[9]

Overpopulation accelerates climate change through the massive use of fossil fuels (necessary to achieve an average of 20 MWh per year per person in the absence of nuclear energy), deforestation for habitat and agriculture, mass livestock farming to meet relentless demand, and intensive agriculture.

Population inflation, or overpopulation, is a consequence of economic insecurity and insufficient education. The less wealthy individuals, without a pension promise, tend to have large families in the hope of securing their old age. That's why we rarely hear about birth control to protect the environment, as it would require wealth redistribution and prioritizing education—goals that policymakers either do not wish to pursue or believe impossible.

To illustrate and mobilize public opinion for their benefit, NGOs, the moral authorities of decision-makers, invented "Earth Overshoot Day," the date when humanity, ever-increasing in number, would have consumed all the planet's renewable resources and would begin drawing from reserves. In 2022, this day fell on July 28, compared to December 25 in 1971.

Experts, often funded by our taxes through the National Institute for Demographic Studies and holding a globalist and pro-immigration ideology, claim that changing lifestyles will solve everything, and that progress will lead African women to have fewer children.

Reality contradicts these claims. Living standards are not improving; rather, they are deteriorating with overpopulation. If education is the solution, more resources will be required as the population grows. Teachers become harder to find as the general population remains poorly educated. When beliefs or ideologies thrive among poorly educated masses, particularly those excluding girls from school, a vicious, difficult-to-break cycle is set in motion.

These experts also propose that Western lifestyles could serve as a reference in other regions, an idea daily disproved by the tensions between the West and emerging countries–a reflection of a clash of civilizations where obscurantism does not seem likely to yield to the myth of universalism.

When individual energy capture is insufficient in some very poor countries, people substitute it with reproduction. Additional individuals providing energy capture allow for cheap labor. Having many descendants also offers a makeshift retirement security that no institutions can guarantee.

In the end, without controlling either the total amount of promise-money or the global population, how can we hope to control price inflation or climate disruption?

After all, limiting births and accepting an aging population is a lesser sacrifice than enduring an austere life on a crowded and depleted planet. It is not about discouraging having children as caricatured by natalists, but simply encouraging women in emerging countries to limit themselves to two children.

Europe has already achieved this, averaging just 1.5 children per woman across the EU. In contrast, in Niger, the average was 6.9 children per woman in 2020, according to the World Bank.

Birth control through encouraging demographic moderation does not seem to be an excessively punitive measure. However, because it would involve women, it is not politically correct. Indeed, the global population at any given time results from two variables: life expectancy and reproductive rate. The alternative to birth control through education and access to contraception is population limitation through wars, epidemics, famines, or even the premature extinction of the species.

Inflation and Debt

"Bitcoin is not a way to get rich quickly; it's a way to avoid becoming poor slowly."

– Jameson Lopp, 2019.

Credit enables unlimited money creation. Here's how it works in practice. When a bank issues a loan, it records two simultaneous entries. First, it notes that Bob owes the bank $10,000 – the loan contract. At the same time, it credits Bob's account with $10,000, effectively creating new money. Bob's account balance represents what the bank owes him, meaning the bank now owes Bob $10,000, while Bob owes the bank the same amount. And voilà! It's magic. The additional $10,000 loaned to Bob can now circulate in the economy. The bank didn't transfer an amount it previously held; it simply created $10,000 with only Bob's promise to repay as collateral.

When Bob makes his $1,000 monthly payment, we see monetary destruction in action: The $1,000 is deducted from his account, reducing the bank's debt to Bob by $1,000. Simultaneously, after the installment payment, Bob's debt also decreases by $1,000.

In practice, new credit issuance consistently outpaces debt repayment, leading to a net expansion of the money supply.

Credit-based money creation far exceeds money destruction from repayments.

This magic of credit-based money creation translates into a rapid increase in the broad money supply (M2, in economists' jargon, consisting of coins, banknotes, and funds in central bank accounts). This is the problem of "magic money," created by the mere will of banks, commonly referred to as "fiat" money ("so be it" in Latin).

Because the quantity of fiat money increases faster than the amount of goods and services exchanged, the prices of these goods and services must constantly adjust and, therefore, rise at a constant energy-value. Wages, being upstream from consumption in the chronology of exchanges, do not increase as quickly. Additionally, the anchoring bias, a well-known psychological phenomenon, prevents businesses from synchronizing the increase in their costs with the increase in their prices. This mismatch leads to a loss of purchasing power for employees.

Technological progress, characterized by productivity gains, must, therefore, compensate for this dilution of value: the endless pursuit of progress is inherent to fiat money.

A central bank doesn't actually have liabilities and owes nothing to anyone. The size of its balance sheet simply represents the amount of energy it has monetized from borrowers. In the context of a monetary creation monopoly, the borrowers consist of all the stakeholders within a monetary zone (defined by the monopoly): public entities, private businesses, and individuals. Each borrower has committed to providing the bank with a portion of their work, that is, their energy, corresponding to their repayments over the duration of the loan.

When the state goes into debt, it is the labor of all taxpayers that is committed to repaying it. Indeed, servicing public debt, which grows dangerously when the cost of money production is negligible for the issuer, relies on taxes and levies.

"Today's debt is tomorrow's tax," to paraphrase, "today's profits are tomorrow's investments."

Inflation and Interest

When central bank borrowing rates drop to zero, banks take advantage using a seemingly foolproof strategy. They borrow cheap money to purchase Treasury bonds, which are issued by a government to finance its policies. These Treasury bonds typically yield very little for their holders. This move is a winning strategy as long as low rates persist, but when central banks suddenly raise their rates, bank failures can occur. This is exactly what happened in the United States in March 2023, when three banks failed within just a few days: Silvergate Bank on March 8, Silicon Valley Bank on March 10, and Signature Bank on March 11.

Indeed, the Treasury bonds held by these banks quickly depreciated because, in a high inflation context, the capital promised at maturity would be worth much less in ten years. As a result, when clients demanded their money back, the banks had to sell these bonds at a loss. This creates a domino effect. If a sufficient number of clients decide to withdraw their funds simultaneously, any bank in the country could find itself short of liquidity.

In such a situation, the central bank can either rescue the banks in crisis by lending them liquidity or let them fail. The Fed chose to rescue, issuing $300 billion within a few days to save just two banks. Imagine the mountain of money the Fed would need to create if all banks sought help simultaneously and if all clients, in a panic, wanted to withdraw their money at the same time. This would lead to a "bank run." Monetary creation would then trigger an inflationary spiral. And without monetary creation, the economy would come to a halt due to bank failures. This is the problem with a monetary monopoly: while claiming to reduce the risks of instability, it actually creates a systemic risk that would not exist with monetary pluralism. The very mechanism meant to provide stability becomes the biggest threat to the system.

11. Money

By traditional definition, money is a metal coin minted by the sovereign authority to serve as a measure of value, a medium of exchanges, and a store of savings – whether gold, silver, or copper money or any legal instrument with the same functions (paper money, bank money).

But there's a more illuminating way to think about it. I propose: "Money is a technology that allows us to spend tomorrow a value we possess today," or, more generally, a technology for transferring value across space and time.

Money must allow for price formation without interference from public or private interests. If it is given other functions, such as some elasticity to finance the welfare state, it degrades its primary role.

Some claim that money is a social consensus, but notice how these two definitions converge, as the consensus is indeed around the use of a technology – yesterday, the melting of precious metals, today moving through digital networks.

Drawing on insights from Satoshi Nakamoto, Bitcoin's creator, and François Roddier, who established the link between money and energy, I'd like to advance a more nuanced definition: Money is a system for representing a quantity of energy in the form of promises or proofs.

Look at how we describe traditional money in our opening definition – "minted by the sovereign authority." This singular phrase reveals an underlying ideology: the presumed necessity of a monopoly on money, a single currency managed by a single institution – the central bank.

Even referring to money in the singular reflects the same cognitive bias or rather the same support, whether deliberate or unconscious, for the status quo and the monopoly. The centralized Euro network succeeded the Franc, carefully avoiding the question of the monopoly. But since the invention of Bitcoin, other networks, more or less decentralized but distinct from the Euro network, have now enabled transactions on the Internet.

The *de facto* monopoly has fallen, but the *de jure* monopoly remains. For how long? In whose interest? In the history of humanity, the monetary monopoly is a recent phenomenon, one that progressively ended monetary pluralism with the birth of central banks in the early 19th century.

The power of monetary creation, described as "sovereign," does not, however, imply a *de facto* monopoly. It is no longer sovereign as it is delegated to an entity, namely the central bank, which is supposed to be independent of the state. The political power is thus now subordinate to the monetary power, not the other way around. If politicians depend on a monetary monopoly to finance their election campaigns and then execute their programs, it is this monopoly that holds the real power.

The Need for Order

Money fundamentally addresses the need for order, first by allowing the assignment of a numerical value to the otherwise subjective value of each thing but also by allowing individuals to hold wealth (or energy) for future use. This second point deserves careful attention, as it implies the freedom to exercise a property right over a certain amount of money. This is not so obvious, as one must be able to ensure the security of their own funds (autonomous storage or self-custody) or entrust them to a third party. However, money entrusted to a well-identified third party becomes confiscable once a superior authority—government or central bank—orders it to freeze the owner's assets.

Bitcoin, by design, is difficult to confiscate, and it is relatively easy to hold or self-custody one's own funds. It is possible to cross a border with millions in value without any detectable sign, simply by memorizing a secret phrase that grants access to a Bitcoin wallet.

The need for order permeates the entire political spectrum, as it can translate into both a need for authority and anarchism, which advocates for an order free from all power. For the most demanding, money must even contribute to a form of harmony, a harmony that Balzac saw as the poetry of order.

Thus, our conceptions of money and religion are not independent but linked by our underlying relationship to that superior and universal force known as energy. Energy possesses all the characteristics of a divine creator in its omnipotence and ubiquity but falls outside the sacred realm, subject to the rigorous scrutiny of science.

Approaching cosmology through the science of energy, the fundamental question seems more about the expression of the rules governing the behavior of energy than about the creation of the universe.

This helps explain why some people call Bitcoin a religion. When I hear this, I understand that the person has vaguely perceived the link between money and religion but has not explicitly identified it as energy. In reality, Bitcoin, due to its decentralized network topology, aligns more with atheism or agnosticism ("rules without rulers") than with the Euro, which mirrors the Catholic Church's centralized hierarchy with its pope and cardinals – the central bank governors.

Two Views of Money

This chapter presents two perfectly consensual theses and two contentious questions, reflecting opposing political visions: providential collectivism and responsible individualism.

The consensual part is straightforward. Money represents energy exchanged in a transaction. It can represent past energy, known as proof-of-value money, or future energy, referred to as promise - based money.

The controversial debates center on two issues: First, should banks maintain their monopoly on monetary creation despite a pluralism of competing currencies? Second, why do we prefer promise - based money over proof-of-value money? The answer lies in how promise - based money enables both the welfare state and imperialism, while proof-of-value money rewards individual labor and responsibility.

Money as Energy

Before we proceed, let's review the key physics concepts that underpin our discussion:

> Mechanical work = force × displacement
> Power = work/time
> Energy = power multiplied by the time during which it is applied.
> Energy and work are equivalent and measured in joules (J).
> Power is measured in watts (W). One joule equals one watt for one second.

When a salary is paid, money represents the energy devoted to work; it then becomes a reserve of energy that the employee can spend in the future to obtain an equivalent amount of energy in value (not necessarily in quantity), notably in the form of a good that itself required energy to be produced.

More generally, a monetary unit corresponds to the "monetization" (more precisely, "tokenization") of energy (power multiplied by the time during which it is applied). Money is used in two main ways: 1) to pay a salary in exchange for work (power exerted over a period), or 2) to purchase an object, whose price combines both its utility (the energy it will help to release or save) and the energy cost of its design, production, and distribution.

For a tangible or intangible good, we can talk about an energy stock. But, for a service, we consider it a flow of energy, namely the work provided in executing the service.

Thousands of years ago, Aristotle's definition of money hinted at this distinction when he discussed a store of value, representing an energy stock, versus a medium of exchange, representing an energy flow.

A monetary system is thus a modeling of the flows and reserves of energy exchanged between humans. For the system to function, the modeling must be consensual among users. In monopolistic systems, this consensus can only be manufactured through manipulation and coercion.

Bitcoin takes a different approach. It creates consensus by linking each monetary value to a verifiable amount of energy spent by miners, who are the validators of transactions on the Bitcoin network, collectively acting as trusted intermediaries. Bitcoin establishes the link between money and energy by relying on the principle of proof-of-work, which combines mathematics (cryptography and game theory) and physics (thermodynamics). We can say that Bitcoin, like gold, verifiably transfers past energy, the energy that was used to produce the coin, into present transactions.

Since each fraction of bitcoin or gold carries its own proof of energy, we can categorize gold and Bitcoin as types of proof-of-value money. Traditional money, like the dollar, works differently. Its association between monetary value and the exchanged energy is ensured by law rather than mathematics. The legal framework (including the monetary and financial code and the status of central banks) mandates central bankers to determine monetary policy, associating a certain amount of fiat money with the amount of energy users need to exchange.

Another known mechanism of energy monetization is at play when a company issues shares. Listed and liquid shares constitute a form of value-based money. S&P500 companies or GAFAM regularly use this form of centralized money to acquire other companies, whether competitors or innovators. As with fiat money, without proof-of-work, the link between a listed share and the underlying energy (the energy represented by the value of the company) is purely legal. A share transfers the company's future profits into the present of a transaction, just as promise-based money transfers the future energy of the borrower.

The Masters of Time

As soon as a future energy is monetized, speculation plays a central role. Speculation is, by nature, the manifestation of a vision of the future. We all speculate, constantly, but on different objects of speculation, with different time horizons.

When an informed saver chooses to keep money in a savings account rather than invest in Bitcoin, they're speculating that Bitcoin will decline more than their (admittedly negligible) savings interest will grow. Two main determinants drive their decision: the perception of risk and the time preference.

What happens when a future energy is monetized? A new object of speculation is created: Will the promisor (the borrower of a new debt or a company issuing new shares) actually deliver that future energy?

To paraphrase a famous quote from Einstein, two world views influence our perception of risk: either nothing happens by miracle, or everything happens by miracle.

Decentralization and Price Stability

Unlike centralized monetary systems, Bitcoin is an autonomous system that does not include a mechanism to adjust its money supply but instead sets a definitive maximum of 21 million units. This is why, as the amount of energy exchanged between users increases, the value represented by a bitcoin increases according to the law of supply and demand, in the same proportions.

Central banks take the opposite approach. Their mandate requires them to ensure price stability expressed in fiat money, forcing them to continuously adjust the money supply. Fiat money is an example of a "stablecoin," that is, a monetary system designed to ensure the stability of the average prices of a certain consumption basket.

If this basket included energy, such as the price of x joules of electricity, there would be a sort of official rate for energy that could diverge from the true market price for energy. This explains why energy is conspicuously absent from the consumption basket set for the Consumer Price Index, which helps governments minimize inflation figures used in civil servant wage negotiations.

The average price of energy paid by Bitcoin miners approaches a global floor price because they are collectively incentivized to consume the cheapest electricity through geographical and regulatory arbitrage to remain profitable.

Aristotle to the Rescue of Central Bankers

The famous definition of money attributed to Aristotle gives the word "money" its status as an anti-concept: money is a system that fulfills three functions—medium of exchange, store of value, and unit of account.

Aristotle outlines the different functions of money but leaves out five fundamental properties, namely scarcity, divisibility, transferability, fungibility, and liquidity.

I don't believe that durability is an interesting or fundamental criterion, as it would only serve to exclude bananas or tulips from the category of money. Metallic or digital currencies are clearly durable. Some have even advocated for melting digital currencies, that is, currencies whose durability is intentionally degraded to discourage saving. Let's say that durability is not universally accepted and set it aside as non-essential.

Scarcity, however, is crucial. It's defined by the amount of energy required to obtain money, either through monetary creation with an energy-backed counterpart in the form of proof or a promise of energy, or through monetary exchange with an energy-backed counterpart in the form of a good or service.

Thus, a currency without an energy counterpart, such as a proof-of-stake currency, is not scarce, even if its promoters decide to limit its supply.

The divisibility of a currency into smaller units is essential for its use as a medium of exchange. Without sufficient divisibility, small transactions could be hindered. This is particularly important for Bitcoin, with its limited quantity and increasing base unit value over time. Some detractors confuse scarcity with divisibility, as the divisibility of the euro, whose value decreases over time, may stop at cents without short-term consequences.

Fiat money, in fact, has a scaling problem rather than a divisibility issue. To mask the effects of inflation, politicians and bankers imposed the switch from the franc to the new franc in 1960 (with a conversion rate of 100 old francs for one new franc), and then the switch from the new franc to the euro in 2002 (with a conversion rate of 6.56

francs for one euro). Without these manipulations, a baguette today would not cost one euro but 656 francs, while the price of a baguette in 1960 was 30 francs!

	Source of energy	Temporality	Proof
Bitcoin	Excess production	Past energy	Mathematics
Gold	Fossil + manual work	Past energy	Physics
Stocks	Company	Future energy	Legal
Fiat Money	Borrower	Future energy	Legal

It's also worth noting that, according to INSEE, "considering monetary erosion due to inflation, the purchasing power of one euro in 2022 is the same as that of 56.40 old francs in 1960," meaning 0.09 €. In other words, fiat money has lost 91% of its value since 1960, but changes in units have allowed this to be hidden from the general public.

Transferability refers to the freedom to instantly send a sum of money to your neighbor or to a third party on the other side of the world. It's a given for digital currency but can be hindered by regulation and, in the case of fiat money, by performance issues linked to monopolistic control.

Fungibility characterizes goods that are consumed through use and can be replaced by goods of the same nature, quality, and quantity. In practical terms, fungibility determines the ability to use bitcoins or euros regardless of their transaction history. Without fungibility, a merchant might refuse payment with a sum of cash on the grounds that it had previously been used for illicit purposes.

Liquidity results from acceptance by a sufficiently large group of users equipped with market infrastructures such as exchanges. The size of this group allows for the quick acquisition or disposal of a significant amount of money.

Liquidity is an intrinsic characteristic of money because, let's recall, the value of money has both an energetic dimension (Yang) and a social dimension (Yin). The number of users determines its social value and liquidity. Users are part of the monetary system in the same way that individuals are part of a species. Dissipative structures are interwoven.

It's worth noting that the use of money as a medium of exchange is primarily conditioned by liquidity. Indeed, in a digital environment, a buyer's Currency A can be instantly exchanged for seller's Currency B, as long as the exchange market between A and B is liquid.

Despite its volatility, Bitcoin can absolutely function as a medium of exchange due to the deep liquidity of bitcoin/euro markets. If this usage remains infrequent, it's because Gresham's law applies (Bitcoin holders prefer to dispose of euros rather than bitcoins in their purchases), but also because merchants are discouraged from accepting Bitcoin under pressure from banks, due to state-imposed tax and accounting complexities.

For its use as a unit of account, it is preferable that the value of the currency in question does not fluctuate too much during the accounting period. However, in a digital environment, converting accounts from one currency to another poses no difficulty; it's the heterogeneity of accounting and tax standards that creates the complexity.

Aristotle's third monetary function – the unit of account– is more debatable because, for central bankers, it implies exclusivity. They readily speak of THE "legal tender." If a currency is used as an exclusive unit of account, it gains a decisive advantage over others and, quite naturally, leads to a monetary monopoly. The non-exclusive unit of account function opens up possibilities for other measures that might diverge from the goal of an exclusive unit of account, namely, price stability expressed in that unit.

In other words, the monopolistic unit of account could give way to a plurality of accounts. A company could thus publish accounts that flourish in euros but are disastrous in carbon footprint, or vice versa. The plurality of currencies and accounts is a prerequisite for responsible corporate governance and informed public policies.

The use of a unit of account is also vulnerable to the wear and tear of time or the volatility of exchange rates. A "stablecoin" is optimized to fulfill this function within a tautological definition that actually combines three systems (monetary, accounting, and fiscal) to form a single reference framework.

Gresham's law tells us that as a medium of exchange, bad money drives out good money. If one currency loses value relative to another, holders will want to get rid of it by using it for purchases and will keep the better currency as a store of value.

The history of gold illustrates the dynamics of these three functions – once a unit of account and medium of exchange, the yellow metal has transformed into a store of value, giving up the medium of exchange role to paper money. Conversely, Bitcoin, which is currently favored for its role as a store of value, could evolve into a global payment network.

The problem with Aristotle's definition is the function of the unit of account, which makes it normative, as accounting serves as the basis for taxation. By explicitly favoring a "stablecoin" over any other form of currency, it implicitly designates a currency recognized by a tax authority. We are approaching the definition of the euro, which probably explains why central bankers often invoke Aristotle to define money in their own way while claiming the authority of his argument.

Bringing everything back to history when discussing innovation, whether monetary or otherwise, is an authoritarian reflex. An authoritarian is uncomfortable with anything that challenges the established order, which, by definition, is precisely what innovation does. They are also uncomfortable with the role of the learner, which is necessary to understand innovation.

Proof-Money and Promise-Money

The public is not invited to debates on monetary systems because those in charge do not want to open Pandora's box by educating the public about how debt-money functions. Thus, instead of democratic discussions, we get epistocratic debates reserved for self-proclaimed and co-opted experts within the "circle of reason" defined by Alain Minc. Ironically, these confidential discussions take place in Davos, on Thomas Mann's Magic Mountain.

Promise-money, issued through credit, represents a borrower's future energy, their promise to repay. It is sometimes described as elastic, given that, in theory, there is no limit to the amount of promise-money that can be created.

The flow of loans and repayments regulates how much promise-money circulates. In contrast, gold and Bitcoin fall into the category of inelastic currencies, whose maximum supply varies little or not at all.

Proof-money works differently. Instead of representing future energy (like a borrower's promise), it represents proof of past energy expenditure. Generally speaking, proof-money is inelastic because the underlying – past energy - cannot be adjusted quickly and arbitrarily to respond to changes in demand.

In the case of Bitcoin or metallic currencies, each unit proves energy was spent to create it. This expended energy gives the currency its fundamental value.

Use Value of Bitcoins

Before being a currency, Bitcoin is a payment network. Its value relies on the necessity of holding bitcoins to use this network, which offers a unique combination of five desirable properties for a payment network:

1. Global reach
2. Censorship resistance (through decentralization)
3. Resilience (no single point of failure)
4. High availability (99.9%+ uptime for 12+ years)
5. Dramatically lower costs than traditional systems

The decentralization of a network is important. No single entity can control it or shut it down, meaning it has no single point of failure or central control. In other words, if a participant leaves the network, it continues to operate as intended, and no one can alter this behavior on their own. This property is essential for a global payment infrastructure like the Bitcoin network. Indeed, in a digitized society, control over payment methods allows for increased surveillance, which can turn into censorship if that control falls into the hands of an authoritarian government.

Regarding costs, the potential savings enabled by the Bitcoin network on payment fees are enormous – around 1 trillion dollars per year for businesses and individuals.[10] According to a recent BCG study, traditional centralized payment networks collect around 1 trillion dollars in fees annually worldwide, compared to 200 million dollars for the Bitcoin network (5,000 times less!). Banks also collect around 1 trillion dollars per year in interest on payments (see the same BCG study).

One might argue that if the number of Bitcoin transactions increases to reach the level of traditional payment methods – several tens of thousands of transactions per second – interest costs would need to be added. But thanks to the speed and efficiencies inherent in Lightning[11] channel protocol, there is no reason for liquidity fees to reach, let alone exceed, such staggering levels.

A promise - money token can also represent a share in a company or a portion of ownership in a property. Its issuance must then be accompanied by a contract or legal framework linking the token to a share or title of ownership. This legal link must rely on a legal entity, which then becomes a centralized point of control.

Bitcoin's decentralization comes from the fact that its value, like that of metallic currency, is free from the need for this legal link. Its decentralization accomplishes three key tasks:

- **Reduces the economic privileges of traditional financial intermediaries**. It allows participants to bypass obligatory gateways. Indeed, anyone can directly participate in the network by issuing transactions and holding their own bitcoins, and they can choose whether to use an intermediary for conservation and payment services.
- **Promotes responsibility rather than risk transfer**, as intermediaries must now convince their clients of the value

added by their services; they can no longer impose one-sided contracts without discussion. Any transfer of responsibility must now be justified.

- **Facilitates access to monetary creation**, as anyone can participate in mining, either directly or through a mining cooperative.[12] Discretionary access to credit, practically reserved for the wealthiest, is no longer the only way to benefit from monetary creation.

With centralized currency, a legal link is established between the token and the underlying energy. The entity holding this contract can be the state or a private company (shares as promise-money).

For a decentralized currency like Bitcoin, in the absence of a legal entity clearly identifying an issuer, this link can only be physical in the form of *proof-of-work*.

A Monopoly of Money?

By prioritizing monetary creation for banks and financial asset holders rather than non-financial economic actors, a monopoly on promise-money introduces a distortion in price formation and access to economic opportunities. It thus fuels sectors that would objectively be deemed unsustainable or harmful from a social, environmental, or economic perspective. Economic actors must be able to freely choose the currency they use, just as they must be able to vote freely.

Currencies are the ballots of the true first round of elections, determining which candidates even appear on the ballot. To be convinced of this, one only needs to see how political parties incur debt to finance their electoral campaigns.

Traditional currencies are geographically and politically defined within a historical framework that is increasingly out of step with the topology of the networks where economic values circulate today. In short, they are marked by technological obsolescence, even as the performance demands of a monetary system continue to rise across all social and economic dimensions. This obsolescence is exacerbated by their traditional network architecture, with a central master point entrenched in its role – the central bank – and enslaved points of presence – the commercial banks – that are not very agile because they are constrained by multiple regulatory requirements.

Aristotle's three functions of money are not exclusive to a monopolistic currency. Different currencies can optimize for different roles. A "stablecoin" is optimal as a unit of account because it is specifically designed to fulfill this function. Bitcoin is optimal as a monetary standard and store of value. The medium of exchange function can be fulfilled by either a "stablecoin" or Bitcoin, as long as both are sufficiently liquid and can be exchanged for each other quasi-instantly in digital transactions.

In reality, in a digital context mediated by machines and code, the function of a medium of exchange depends less on monetary policy than on the liquidity of the currency in question within a network of acceptance.

The two categories of currency, proof-money and promise-money, that we have defined must be able to coexist to create competition between currencies for the benefit of users rather than forcing individuals to compete for money. This vision offers not just one economy but intertwined economies, fostering greater resilience and prosperity.

Europe could make the euro more attractive than the U.S. dollar by mitigating the risk of sanctions and confiscation, thus promoting the euro as a reserve currency. Bitcoin takes this logic to its extreme by offering an apolitical currency. The euro misses this opportunity because European institutions are politically powerless in the face of the technological vassalization exerted by the United States.

In his 1936 short story "The Invisible Collection," Stefan Zweig tells the story of a collector who, after becoming blind, has his collection of prints sold by those around him and replaced with blank sheets. For central banks, we have become blind collectors, unable to see that their currency no longer has an energy-backed counterpart. This truth occasionally slips out, as when Federal Reserve Chairman Jerome Powell told CBS in May 2020: "We print [money] digitally. As a central bank, we have the ability to create money digitally, and we do so by buying Treasury bills or bonds or other government-guaranteed securities."

If promise-money's energy counterpart is a repayment promise, what happens when repayment becomes unlikely? The counterpart diminishes or even disappears entirely.

Beyond a certain level of improbability, debt repayment becomes a fiction, leading to discussions of "magic money" and even questioning the necessity of taxes. If the state can finance itself without limits through debt, the collection of taxes becomes symbolic and serves only to assert public power through wealth redistribution.

Without the safeguard of an energy standard like gold or Bitcoin, monetary creation becomes completely unrestrained. Between 1971 and 2018, the U.S. dollar supply increased thirtyfold, while the dollar price of an ounce of gold increased fiftyfold. When the dollar was convertible into gold, an ounce of gold was worth $35, whereas today, it is worth around $2,000.

In contrast to promise-money, which can be created in potentially unlimited quantities, the three advantages of an inelastic currency like Bitcoin have been convincingly described by Saifedean Ammous in *The Bitcoin Standard*. Firstly, it helps reduce time preference, as the present value is higher than the future value of a good or service, and secondly, it provides a unit of account for price formation.

Like the USSR government, central banks engage in centralized price planning or, at the very least, distort natural price formation mechanisms. When monetary creation encourages corporate offshoring, the savings consumers see in stores are offset by higher taxes and debt repayment, destabilizing the economy. In other words, we pay back what we save at checkout through fiscal burdens, taxes, and debt repayment. Capitalism only works if the capital markets function without distortions, yet bank-driven monetary creation distorts this market.

Capitalism does not scale with promise-money monopolies for three key reasons:

- Access to capital is biased toward size and wealth to the detriment of innovators, new entrants, and local actors.

- The shares of large companies are liquid, while those of small companies are not. The shares of listed companies become a form of promise-money (future profits) with which they can buy unlisted ones. The blind spot in the critique of capitalism lies in failing to first critique the monopolistic promise-based monetary system.

- Inelastic currencies protect individuals from despotism, repression, and imperialism. Elastic promise-money is the essential element in the arms race.

Inspired by Bitcoin's proof-of-work but swayed by the media's misunderstanding of energy issues, some have proposed a monetary system with no direct energy cost, a proof-of-stake (PoS) currency. Proof-of-stake currency, like fiat money, is issued without direct costs for the issuer. There is no need for hardware investments or electricity negotiations. It can be created in unlimited quantities, with all the negative environmental consequences associated with the unchecked monetary expansion in the race for progress.

Proof-of-stake cryptocurrencies are marketed as "green" because they do not directly monetize energy. In contrast, Bitcoin is often portrayed as harmful to the environment simply because it monetizes energy. This framing is misleading:

Energy cannot be created or destroyed; it can only be transformed into another form of energy. This is the first principle of thermodynamics, the science of energy. Lavoisier reinforced this principle of conservation when he stated, "Nothing is lost, nothing is created, everything is transformed." Energy is not consumed; it is used. The word "consumption" applied to energy is misleading; "energy use" is more accurate.

Some argue that certain uses of energy are legitimate while others are wasteful, but this mindset is nothing short of totalitarianism. Bitcoin converts electricity into proof-of-work and dissipated heat. YouTube uses more energy than Bitcoin. Is one more useful than the other? No one can say. An open, global, censorship-resistant payment network that is available 24/7 is as useful as a global video *streaming* network.

Deciding for oneself what is useful and what is not is a fundamental freedom. Utility and value are concepts relative to the observer, not absolutes dictated by an elite. The utility of a good or service can be measured by the amount of energy saved or released by that good or service. The utility of a plow can be measured by the additional energy a farmer would have to expend to plow their field without it.

Bitcoin's scarcity is directly tied to the energy required to mine it. Conversely, currencies that do not monetize energy can be created in unlimited quantities because their production costs are near zero. An unlimited quantity of money leads to the financing of more and more projects, with diminishing returns, until natural resources are exhausted.

Bitcoin mining also establishes a floor price for electricity because miners must find the cheapest electricity to remain profitable. Neither human labor nor electricity is easily transportable or storable.

In a proof-of-stake network, controlling the majority of validators requires an accumulation of tokens. However, the majority of validators are never required to sell their tokens. In contrast, proof-of-work networks remain open to new participants; anyone can secure hardware and negotiate electricity contracts to compete in mining. Thus, one can always attempt to challenge the majority of miners without needing anyone's permission.

A proof-of-stake network is vulnerable to the silent accumulation of tokens, where an entity gradually amasses tokens and eventually gains definitive control of the network, as no one can force the majority validators to sell. This type of attack, which can permanently compromise the decentralization of a PoS network, is impossible on a PoW network. If a miner or group of miners becomes the majority due to their computing power, it is always possible to surpass them by gathering enough hardware and electricity.

Moreover, governance in a proof-of-stake network does not necessarily require an absolute majority due to abstention. Many holders of proof-of-stake tokens do not participate in staking or may abstain from voting on decisions, making it easier for a coordinated minority to dominate. Finally, PoW protocols can enhance the profitability of investments in renewable energy by monetizing the inherent surpluses in energy flows, strengthening the economic viability of renewables in ways PoS cannot.

12. Progress

Technological progress, which frees human time through maximized energy capture, is a direct consequence of the third law of thermodynamics. However, as raw materials are depleted and environmental destruction accelerates, progress itself has become a central topic.

The third law also inevitably leads to the extinction of the species, at the latest by the eventual disappearance of its habitat, the planet Earth, in four billion years. Even the sun's eventual death is an energy fluctuation governed by thermodynamic principles. The causal connection between these two phenomena, progress and extinction, through the same physical principle, should help refute the misguided ways of the primitivists. Indeed, they want to convince us that the headlong rush in which humanity is engaged is not natural and that technological progress is the foundation of a suicidal society.

In reality, the third law guides us on this path to a fatal outcome. A rational approach acknowledges the inevitability of this path but seeks to extend humanity's four-billion-year deadline – a rather ambitious and motivating goal – rather than undermine the technological foundations that will allow us to reach it.

The individual, subject to the third law as a converter, will struggle to change personal habits but can align with the broader goal of technological progress. From this perspective, information technologies, by prioritizing the reduction of entropy before increasing energy capture, are an asset, not the scourge neo-Luddites claim.

Productivism is not an ideology to combat but a physical phenomenon to manage, like floods or droughts. Many activists fail to gain traction in critiquing technology because they misunderstand this fundamental truth.

The only acceptable adjustment in the pursuit of a sustainable way of life is birth control, and here's why. Progress creates machines that free up time and lead to an increase in life expectancy. Humans are no longer exhausted by a lifetime of work and have more time to devote to their health and well-being. Machines use energy, and the amount of energy used is directly linked to the population. The alternative to birth control is population control through the threat of famines and armed conflicts over scarce resources.

To reach a consensus on these issues, archaic religious doctrines that once encouraged high birth rates must be reconsidered. When Genesis commanded, "*Be fruitful and multiply*," the world was sparsely populated. When the Quran emerged around 700 CE, the Earth was about 30 times less populated than it is today. Women's literacy universally correlates with declining birth rates, which is why the most toxic dogmas advocate excluding women from the educational system and marrying them off in childhood. Those who downplay overpopulation are, in reality, ecocidal. Indeed, extrapolations generally underestimate the effects of the law of diminishing returns, which affects both agriculture and the extraction of raw materials. Intensive agriculture and recycling will not offset the pressures of unchecked growth.

The following equation, attributed to Yoichi Kaya, illustrates why population control is a crucial ecological issue:

GHG = (GHG/E) x (E/GDP) x (GDP/POP) x POP

GHG: total quantity of greenhouse gases emitted by human activities

E: total amount of energy used by human activities

GDP: total production of goods and services measured in currency

POP: world population

The GHG/E ratio is very difficult to modify because we observe that new energy sources (renewables) are added to the existing ones (fossil fuels) without ever replacing them. And all indications are that fossil fuels will be exploited until the last accessible drop is used. Likewise, the E/GDP ratio is almost invariant because, as we previously noted regarding the principle of conservation, real GDP and energy used are in a proportional relationship.

Only an improvement in the efficiency of energy transformation by machines could change the E/GDP ratio. However, better efficiency does not encourage a reduction in energy consumption but rather accelerates mechanization to produce even more. This leaves GDP per capita (GDP/POP) and population (POP) as the only truly controllable factors. The GDP/POP ratio, also known as GDP per capita, can decrease if the standard of living is deliberately lowered, which is possible in the wealthiest and least populated countries. However, any decrease will be largely offset by even a slight increase in the poorest and most densely populated countries.

That leaves POP as the only reliable long-term solution. Population can be effectively managed if birth control maintains an average of two children per woman, a threshold that would stabilize global population levels.

Some downplay the impact of overpopulation on greenhouse gas emissions and avoid describing its consequences for humans, namely a reduction in the standard of living, whether in terms of housing, food, or the environmental consequences of the destruction required to exploit ever more land. In emerging countries, famine and armed conflicts are the violent alternatives to peaceful birth control. The use of nitrogen fertilizers in agriculture must keep pace with population growth; however, soil bacteria transform these fertilizers into nitrous oxide (N_2O). Nitrous oxide is a greenhouse gas (GHG) with a global warming potential (GWP) over 100 years that is 300 times greater than an equivalent mass of carbon dioxide.[13]

Even more concerning is the potential shortage of essential metals for transportation and construction to meet the demands of an ever-growing population. Indeed, the efficiency of mineral extraction decreases significantly over time, and the energy expenditure to extract the ore is tenfold when ten times more ore needs to be processed to obtain the same amount of metal, not to mention the expanding land footprint of mines, encroaching on forested or arable land. Copper ore, for example, contains between 0.3% and 2% copper. In an average gold mine, one gram of gold is recovered per ton of ore.

Design, manufacturing, communication, and marketing all depend on demographics and resources. Growth in profits, population growth, and environmental destruction are inseparable.

Natalism, globalism, and immigrationism interpret the word "progress" as an increase in the amount of energy transformed by humans, as an increase in the quantity of life rather than the quality of life. Progress and overpopulation are thus intimately linked in a vicious cycle, with progress enabling an increase in life expectancy. The lengthening of life expectancy motivates reproduction in poor countries, where there is neither social protection nor a pension system. Uncontrolled reproduction combined with migration multiplies the individuals available to feed the god of progress.

Just as we build dams to control rivers, we must regulate birth rates in poor countries to counteract thermodynamic forces. This is not ideology; it's physics. Rationality is intelligence in pursuit of optimal solutions. Unfortunately, it is incompatible with the current methods of selecting public policies, as Gurwinder Bogal observed:

> *The only way to ensure that our intelligence serves reason is to be humble and curious. Unfortunately, humility and curiosity are rare in politics because they are not qualities that win elections. Research has shown that people who talk a lot, even if they have no idea what they are talking about, tend to be chosen by others as leaders.*

Character is what separates intelligence seeking a practical solution from intelligence that is self-centered on achieving personal and irrational goals. Humility and curiosity are indeed the two traits, Yin and Yang, that will form this character. Humility (Yin) fuels our curiosity by preserving the ability to question our beliefs and behaviors, and curiosity (Yang) sustains humility by constantly placing us in a learning situation. These twin virtues – Yin and Yang – must shape leadership if humanity is to navigate the challenges ahead.

13. Promise

Promise: "The act of promising; what one commits to do."

The euro is a form of promise-money, issued in exchange for a promise of repayment by a borrower. Yet, the scale of these promises has rendered them meaningless.

France's public debt soared from 70 billion euros in 1978 to three trillion euros in 2023. In 2021, there were 39.3 million tax households in France, 44% of which paid income tax. When factoring in public sector pension obligations, the actual debt reaches 5 trillion euros or nearly 300,000 euros of debt per taxable household. In other words, the promise of repayment has become a fiction maintained by political and financial decision-makers.

Without the financiers who have taken care to gain control of the media by becoming their shareholders or major advertisers, the public would become aware of the root of its problems – the decoupling between their work and the promise - money they receive in return. This collective awareness is further stifled by leftist critiques of capitalism, the political left's stock-in-trade, which is an objective ally of the central banks' monopoly. Yet, the excesses of capitalism are a consequence, not the cause, of the monetary monopoly.

The political left, fixated on critiquing capitalism, unwittingly reinforces central bank dominance. In reality, capitalism's worst excesses stem from the monetary monopoly, not the free market itself. True capitalism and monopoly rarely coexist, but European institutions have managed to merge the worst aspects of both systems. For example, they have decreed the end of the monopoly on rail transport, even though it is already in competition with other means of transportation. But, they see no problem with the monopoly of a monetary system.

In contrast to the Euro, Bitcoin is a proof-money, issued in exchange for electronic mining energy. In the 21st century, electricity has become dominant in the economy, with electric motors having supplanted steam engines and internal combustion engines. Bitcoin allows us to objectively decide what should or should not be produced with this now universal form of energy.

The market price of a good expressed in bitcoins must be higher than the value (also expressed in bitcoins) of the electricity needed to produce it. Promise-money ends up supporting activities that do not necessarily create wealth and do not free up usable energy.

Bitcoin acts as a filter. It reveals economic activity by aligning energy transformation with wealth creation and ensures that the energy used produces more energy in return.

In other words, in an economy that is almost entirely digitized (electrified), Bitcoin helps create equilibrium between the capacity to convert energy into electricity and the capacity of electric machines (computers, robots, etc.).

So, should we place proof-money and promise-money in opposition or as points along a spectrum of trust that ranges from Bitcoin's "Don't trust, verify" to the euro's dependence on belief and coercion?

14. Rarity

Rarity: "The characteristic of being rare, not widespread, not numerous: rarity of a commodity." Synonyms: insufficiency, lack, shortage. The characteristic of something that happens or occurs infrequently. The quality of being uncommon, unusual.

This definition, is tautological. It is also possible to define rarity as a thermodynamic property: the rarity of something reflects the amount of energy that must be mobilized to get it.

A gold coin is rare because prospecting, extracting the ore, and minting the coin all require a lot of energy. A lot compared to what? Rare compared to what? Rarity, like utility and entropy, is a relative concept that depends on observation and its context.

What is rare carries proof of energy. The potential energy of the material is not enough to characterize rarity. Rather, it is because the material in question is difficult to find (proof of exploration energy) or to recover (proof of physical extraction energy) that it is rare.

Rarity can be expressed mathematically: $\mathbf{R = uE + vS}$

R is rarity. E is the energy required to extract the observed material. u and v are variables (dependent on the material and its macroscopic state), and S is the lack of information about the presence of the material (entropy) that determines the energy of exploration.

Like all information, rarity thus contains a dose of proof (of energy) and a dose of promise (linked to entropy).

From complexity arises uniqueness. Human society is not an anthill. Ants belong to homogeneous categories (worker, soldier, etc.) with relatively predictable behaviors, but humans each possess a degree of rarity. The variable *u* characterizes the macroscopic state of the observed system and, in the case of humans, their individual uniqueness. This link between complexity and rarity is also found at the elemental level. Simple atoms like hydrogen are much more abundant compared to complex atoms like rare earth elements (lanthanum, yttrium, scandium).

The same principle applies to gold. Gold panned from the Amazon is not equally rare as gold mined from the ore in a South African mine. To calculate its rarity, one would need to make a weighted average based on the quantities extracted by these two methods. However, because panning produces negligible amounts, its impact on overall gold rarity is minimal.

The concept of rarity, like any abstraction, can be used for manipulation for commercial purposes. Some speak of rarity in the context of proof-of-stake digital currencies, suggesting a similarity that does not exist with proof-of-work. Proof-of-work represents exploration and extraction of energy, which, as we have just seen, characterizes rarity. However, proof-of-stake does not represent energy, which its promoters even highlight as an ecological virtue. There is no rarity for proof-of-stake currencies because, even if the quantity of currency may be limited on a blockchain, the number of proof-of-stake blockchains is unlimited.

Indeed, a proof-of-stake blockchain is an infrastructure without associated investment or maintenance costs. Each new iteration claims superiority over its predecessors, often boasting higher transaction capacity to compensate for congestion on older chains, which is why they multiply so rapidly.

In reality, the global quantity of proof-of-stake currency, without an energy counterpart, cannot claim the rarity that requires the representation of energy through proof-of-work. This unrestricted replication undermines any claim to rarity.

In contrast, proof-of-work currencies derive their rarity from energy investment. The computational power securing the Bitcoin network (around 500 EH/s at the time of writing) makes a bitcoin much rarer than a litecoin (750 TH/s at the same time). More precisely, assuming the simplified hypothesis that the computing power of the Litecoin network is based on circuits (Antminer L7)[14] using 361,000 Joules per TH, we can estimate the computing power of the Litecoin network to be 750 x 361,000 J/s = 270 MW.

Similarly, assuming that the computing power of Bitcoin is based on circuits (Antminer S19 XP) with an energy efficiency of 21.50 J/TH, we estimate the computing power of the Bitcoin network to be around 500 x 21.50 MJ/s = 10,750 GW.

With these assumptions, the computing power of the Bitcoin network would be 40 times greater than that of Litecoin.[15] In other words, the Bitcoin network is 40 times rarer, according to our energy-based definition of rarity, than the Litecoin network. Knowing that the cumulative value of bitcoins is 200 times higher than that of Litecoins, we can draw two conclusions.

Firstly, the energy dimension of the Bitcoin network alone does not suffice to explain this discrepancy; its social dimension (size of the ecosystem, number of independent nodes, etc.) must also be considered when comparing it to other systems.

Secondly, it seems much more profitable to clone the Bitcoin network or to mine on the Bitcoin network than on the Litecoin network if a 40 times higher cost creates 200 times more value. Of course, this apparent incentive can be questioned by game theory, but it clearly highlights Bitcoin's advantage over any other network operating with proof-of-work.

To be thorough on this thorny issue, we must acknowledge that the social dimension of these networks, beyond their energy dimension, is difficult to measure. Only Bitcoin and, to a much lesser extent, Ethereum have acquired the status of global social networks, in addition to their physical network infrastructure. Most other cryptocurrencies survive thanks to the marketing efforts and price manipulations of their founders.

Bitcoin's combination of thermodynamic rarity (energy), social rarity (adoption), and immutability makes it unique. Other PoW networks struggle to compete, and PoS networks, with their infinite reproducibility, **cannot claim true rarity at all.**

15. Speculation

Speculation: "An operation consisting of buying a good with the aim of making a profit from its later resale."

The word speculation carries such negative connotations that it has also come to mean "abstract construction, arbitrary and unverifiable commentary," synonymous with conjecture.

Definitionally, speculation can refer to an investment, just as manipulation sometimes replaces persuasion. Only intention or context distinguishes their meaning. Investment is traditionally viewed as a long-term endeavor, while speculation is often seen as short-sighted and predatory.

Yet, if time preference is defined as the perceived difference between the present value and the future value of a good or service, there is no threshold of time preference that would allow us to distinguish an investor from a speculator. Both use information to bet on future outcomes.

Speculators are, in fact, investors like any other, using the information at their disposal to bet on a future outcome. For example, if you have studied the functioning of traditional fiat monies, you have observed that their circulating supply increases significantly year after year.

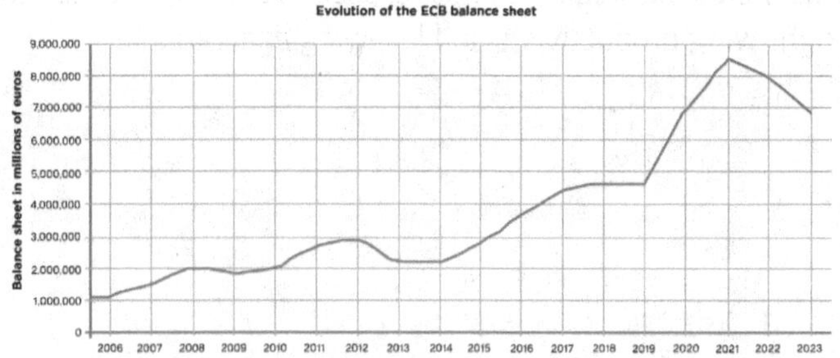

You can, therefore, bet that they will depreciate over time and instead choose to invest in an asset that will appreciate due to its rarity combined with utility. Speculation involves discerning what will be useful over a more or less distant time horizon, which depends on the speculator.

Orthodox economists distinguish between public and private debt, claiming that the state has an infinite lifespan (guaranteed by public institutions), while households and businesses have finite lifespans. The public treasury can, therefore, constantly refinance public debt, a process commonly referred to as "rolling over the debt," making repayment seem unnecessary.

However, this assumption is questionable, as numerous cases of state bankruptcy have shown that the value of a national promise-money can drop to zero. Among others, this occurred in Weimar Republic Germany in 1923, in Latin America (notably Argentina, Bolivia, Brazil, and Chile) in the 1970s and 80s, and in Zimbabwe in 2008.

In reality, when a central bank's debt exceeds the threshold beyond which repayment becomes highly unlikely, it turns into a fiction. A fiction that must be maintained and should only be scrutinized by economists appointed by those central banks. Central bankers carefully avoid talking about their debt and prefer the term "balance sheet," even though it mainly consists of liabilities. In their minds, they owe nothing to anyone, even though they have monetized the future energy of an entire country for decades, if not centuries. Ultimately, if money can be created for the state *ad libitum* and *ex nihilo*, taxes are no longer a financial necessity but rather an incentive for taxpayers to continue producing wealth. In this respect, maintaining taxes satisfies both right-wing productivists and left-wing egalitarians.

Postage stamp with a face value of 5,000 marks modified to 2 million marks (Weimar Republic)

A state can only ensure a stable national promise-money if it lives in autarky or has absolute sovereignty. Historically, only empires like the United States or China have been able to meet these conditions for prolonged periods. A neutral country like Switzerland may also be capable of this as long as it maintains its sovereignty.

Hyman Minsky classified the financing of investments through debt into three types:

1. Hedge Financing: The return on the investment covers both the principal and the interest.

2. Speculative Financing: The return only covers the interest, with the principal of the debt constantly being rolled over.

3. Ponzi Financing: The return does not even cover the interest, and the debt continually increases to meet interest payments.

The United States housing market in the 2000s provided an example of Ponzi financing. An American household could take out a mortgage to purchase a home, but also borrow to pay the monthly installments by using the future appreciation of the property as collateral.

The speculator's discernment determines their success because rarity and utility are relative notions, highly dependent on context and timing. Water is generally abundant in our regions but rare in the desert. A pair of skis is useful to a skier but of no interest to someone who doesn't like the mountains. A carriage was useful in the 19th century, much less so after the adoption of the automobile.

Speculation is, therefore, the exact opposite of gambling, where bets are purely random. Chance has no memory, so there is no effective betting strategy at the gaming table. The expected return in a casino is negative because the casino needs to make a profit.

In contrast, speculation is rooted in research and foresight. Thanks to technological progress, the expected return is positive for astute speculators who have done their homework. Critics, however, equate speculation with social irresponsibility, claiming it prioritizes the detestable pursuit of individual profit at the expense of the collective good.

This convenient alternation between a critique and its opposite (heads I win, tails you lose) is the hallmark of totalitarian rhetoric. It is particularly evident in debates about retirement savings, where opponents denounce the risks while labeling capitalists as profiteers. Yet, if a capitalist takes risks and loses in the stock market, they also lose the status of profiteer. And if they win every time, everyone should play that game, including future retirees. In reality, the critiques are valid, but not for the usual reasons cited about the evils of capitalism.

The problem does not stem from capitalism but from the monopoly of promise-money. By allocating monetary creation through credit to the wealthiest, the monetary monopoly rigs the game of speculation by reserving it for a plutocracy. The plutocrat not only reduces entropy in price formation but also increases it with their own liquidity, artificially inflated by credit, which can influence prices upwards.

Additionally, the wealthiest players can socialize their losses, thereby protecting themselves from real risk. This euphemism, also known as "too big to fail," allows large institutions to absorb unlimited credit (money creation), reaching a critical size where their failure is deemed a systemic risk, forcing bailouts at taxpayers' expense.

The use of the word *speculation* is thus doubly suspect. It carries a moral judgment on those who seek profit, even though it is an essential cog in the price formation mechanism. It also implies an unspoken desire for the arbitrary predetermination of what will be useful and rare, which resembles a planned economy. As philosopher Roger Scruton writes, "Some intellectuals are naturally drawn to the idea of a planned society because they believe they will be in charge of it."

Price formation corresponds to a reduction in entropy, which leads to an increase in the energy flow for all economic agents. In this respect, the speculator who participates in price formation performs a socially useful function, even if it is sometimes morally questionable.

Unfortunately, the monopoly of promise-money ends up making capitalism resemble a planned economy by granting an oligarchy preferential access to credit and thus to monetary creation. As a result, there is no longer fair access to capital.

The critique of speculation seems to be based on the excesses of capitalism but fails to address the true culprit: the monopoly of promise-money.

16. Utility

Utility: 1) The fact of being useful for something. 2) The characteristic or quality of something or someone that serves a purpose: The telephone is of great utility. 3) The aptitude of a good to satisfy a need or to create favorable conditions for this satisfaction.

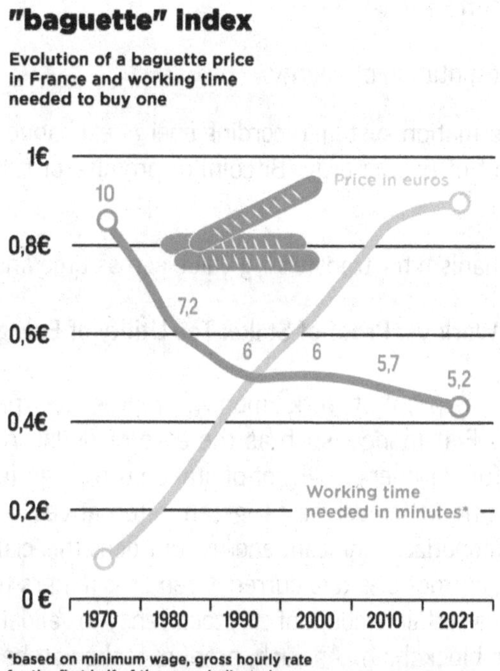

The "Baguette Index" represents the amount of work time necessary to buy a baguette. It makes explicit the intuitive link between the cost of a good or service and a quantity of energy. Indeed, work time is related to the amount of energy used at a given power by the equation Power = Energy / Time.

At this point, some readers might object that the power of work varies from one individual to another, and they would be correct. Work time is an approximation, whereas the amount of energy is a more precise measure. However, work time expressed in minutes is a much more relatable concept for most of us than a quantity of energy expressed in joules, making the Baguette Index a useful pedagogical tool.

The science of energy is a source of inspiration for rethinking economic principles. Let's examine how this allows us to reformulate the definition of utility to make it measurable. Work is a flow of mechanical energy. By aligning money, work, and energy, we can reformulate currency as:

- A representation of energy
- An information system recording energy exchange in the form of proof of past energy (Bitcoin) or promise of future energy (credit)
- A mechanism for transferring value across time and space

Proof-of-Work vs. Proof-of-Stake: The Utility of Energy

Bitcoin, as proof-of-work money, represents past energy expenditure. Fiat money, such as the euro or dollar, represents a promise of future energy. Proof-of-stake currencies (e.g., Solana, Cardano) position themselves as "green" alternatives, arguing that they do not monetize significant energy. But does this claim hold up?

Typically, a proof-of-stake currency requires miners to prove the possession of a certain amount of cryptocurrency to validate additional blocks in the blockchain. As such, proof-of-stake can be seen as an energy-proof that requires no actual energy, except for the negligible amount needed to calculate signatures. In this way, it is similar to fiat money, which is a promise of energy. But, without proof of past energy, promises of future energy can be created in unlimited quantities. These currencies favor short-term thinking and unlimited consumption rather than frugality and investment.

Generally, inflation encourages savers to "get rid" of their cash reserves as quickly as possible by making investments of all kinds, including short-term ones. Unlimited monetary creation leads to the financing of an unlimited number of projects, with the progressive depletion of natural resources.

In contrast, Bitcoin's proof-of-work allows for limited monetary creation, which is conducive to long-term investments. The increasing value of rare currency frees investors from concerns about hyperinflation, a characteristic of currencies created in unlimited quantities. They can, therefore, more calmly focus on financing sustainable projects.

Fiat monies are corrupted forms of money because banks prioritize already creditworthy borrowers. The greater the borrower's wealth measured in euros, the more credit (monetary creation) they can access. Moreover, bank credit is also distributed at the banks' discretion, forming a network of influence.

If a representation of energy is a form of information, what distinguishes information from a quantity of energy? Information differs from energy simply in that it is replicable. If I share information, I still have it after sharing it, whereas energy is not replicable. A bitcoin, protected by the network's energy barrier against double-spending, comes closest to a form of non-replicable energy while remaining digital information.

Just as a catalyst is found at the end of a catalytic chemical reaction, information is found at the end of an energy transformation involving entropy reduction. In chemistry, a catalyst is a substance that increases the speed of a chemical reaction; it participates in the reaction but is neither a product nor a reactant, and, therefore, does not appear in the overall equation of the reaction.

Information is the thermodynamic equivalent of a chemical catalyst. It facilitates (accelerates) work (energy flow) and allows for energy savings without being part of the energy balance. The information remains intact at the end of the energy transformation. For example, the assembly instructions for a piece of flat-pack furniture help speed up the assembly work, i.e., the energy flow, but remain available to assemble another piece of the same furniture.

Digital currency isn't a raw material, as raw materials store energy through nuclear energy in atoms, molecular binding energy, gravitational potential energy, and more generally, any additional energy resulting from an interaction force. Barter is an exchange of energy stocks, whereas a monetary exchange involves information that represents energy. This information is *useful* because the one who uses it benefits from a transfer of energy in space and/or time. After the monetary transaction, the information representing the energy still exists and thus requires a mechanism to prevent double-spending, i.e., either a centralized bank ledger or a decentralized network like Bitcoin.

The utility of a good or service is measured by the amount of energy that can be saved or released by that good or service. For example, the utility of a plow is the difference between the energy used by the farmer to plow his field with the plow and the energy he would have had to expend to do the same without the plow. This represents energy saved. Utility is the primary determinant of the price of the plow because it sets a ceiling in case of scarcity. If there is an abundance of plows, their price may fall below this ceiling. The manufacturing cost represents the stocks and flows of energy used in the manufacturing process and sets a floor for the price, which will fluctuate between the cost (floor) and utility (ceiling). These fluctuations are dictated by the law of supply and demand, which is itself subject to the power dynamics between buyers and sellers.

Utility is always relative. Like the utility of an umbrella, it can take on negative values depending on the context.

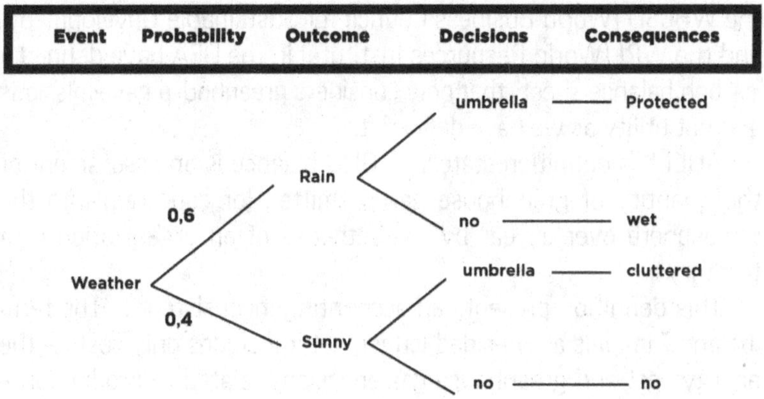

Bitcoin is economically useful as a monetary system with properties that differentiate it from traditional debt-based currency systems, such as its resistance to censorship and its limited supply. But its utility extends beyond finance. It is also socially useful because it indirectly sets a global floor price for energy flows, renewable energy, and labor.

Of course, Bitcoin's use of energy invites misleading comparisons from proponents of the status quo. Yet, banking systems, gold mining, and data centers like those of Google and YouTube all use more energy than Bitcoin. The difference? These systems operate in regions of high energy demand, whereas Bitcoin miners can only remain profitable by seeking out the lowest-cost energy.

Indeed, the data centers of banks must be located near densely populated areas where energy demand is already high, whereas Bitcoin miners engage in geographic arbitrage, setting up operations in areas where production surpluses exist. These surpluses only appear with an energy flow (renewable) because the sale of an energy stock (fossil) can always be deferred to sell it when demand is highest. By monetizing these energy surpluses, Bitcoin secures a global floor price for renewable energy, enhancing the prospect of investments in this sector.

Finally, it should be noted that the notion of a carbon footprint, often brandished by so-called environmentalists, is often incomplete. The ADEME (Environment and Energy Management Agency) in France, the WBCSD (World Business Council for Sustainable Development), and the WRI (World Resources Institute) in the USA have defined a "carbon balance sheet" that only considers greenhouse gas emissions and not utility as we have defined it.

ADEME's definition states: "A GHG balance is an assessment of the quantity of greenhouse gases emitted (or captured) into the atmosphere over a year by the activities of an organization or a territory."

This definition presents an accounting inconsistency. The term "balance" implies a two-sided ledger, yet it includes only costs – the energy cost and greenhouse gas emissions related to production – while omitting the energy saved or released (utility) by the activities in question. For example, Bitcoin, as a substitute for gold, could save the cost of gold mining, which is much more polluting. Excluding the "utility" column from the carbon balance excludes utility from the debate, thus arbitrarily deciding what is useful to society and what is not, according to their agenda.

And if utility is subjective, who has the right to define it? It takes a totalitarian logic to dictate to everyone what is useful or not. If the dictator is not a fan of skiing, he will decree that ski slopes and lifts are useless. The same logic applies to monetary systems.

If the monetary monopoly were truly as virtuous as its defenders claim, why is it never up for debate? The silence suggests that an oligarchy has gradually entrenched itself with the advent and development of central banks and the modern banking system, eliminating the competition of currencies that existed for millennia.

Because I cannot vote on the monetary system itself, Bitcoin has become my means of dissent–a tool to express disagreement with a system that does not align with my worldview. Beyond personal expression, Bitcoin is also practical. It enables faster, cheaper international transactions than traditional banking, and it provides protection against arbitrary asset confiscation and inflation in countries where monetary instability threatens financial sovereignty. Bitcoin's utility is not theoretical. It is real, tangible, and increasingly necessary in a world where monetary and financial control is concentrated in fewer hands than ever before.

Finally, and most importantly, Bitcoin would be useless if the euro were a perfect currency whose perfection was unsurpassable. Otherwise, Bitcoin is useful because it is different and offers an alternative and open system. In other words, since the euro is imperfect, Bitcoin cannot be perfectly useless and may even be perfectly useful.

So, what are the imperfections of the euro?

1. **Structural inefficiency**. The direct costs and opportunity costs of its inefficient organization ("labor-intensive"). The euro mobilizes more than 300,000 full-time jobs in France, with higher pay than in other sectors, even as productive professions struggle to recruit due to unattractive wages. In France alone, the financial sector extracts over 100 billion euros per year from non-financial industries – a monopoly rent rather than a reflection of genuine cost - benefit balance.

2. **Credit allocation inequity**. Banks favor lending to large corporations and the wealthy, reinforcing wealth concentration among those who already hold significant assets. Redistribution through taxation does little to counteract this, as the Laffer curve[16] suggests diminishing returns on excessive taxation.

3. **Arbitrary credit distribution**. The Cantillon effect ensures that those closest to monetary issuance benefit first. Bankers determine which company or political party will be funded at the expense of others. They handpick an ecosystem of dependents who, in turn, reinforce the system through regulatory capture.

4. **Fragility of centralization**. A monetary system dependent on a single point of failure–whether a central bank or political entity – is inherently vulnerable.

5. **Monetary expansion and overconsumption**. A currency that can be created without limit (promise-money) encourages excess borrowing and spending, leading to speculative bubbles, malinvestment, and resource depletion.

This last point should be offset by the effects of technological progress, even if these are preempted by monetary creation. But, public power is boosted by exponential monetary creation to deal with system crises. Each crisis begets new rounds of monetary expansion, creating a vicious feedback loop that can only be broken by ending the monopoly on money creation. Technological progress can be defined as an increase in our ability to capture free energy. In the case of Bitcoin, the energy it uses is clearly less than the energy it would allow to be liberated. In 2020, 2.2 million jobs in the EU were dedicated to the functioning of the traditional banking system.[17] Many of these jobs could be redeployed, at least in part, to essential activities such as education (1.45 million university teachers in 2021)[18] or healthcare (14 million workers).

The value of a good or service combines two components: its rarity and its utility. The amount of energy required for its creation, in other words, the difficulty of obtaining it, defines its rarity; the amount of energy it saves represents its utility. Bitcoin's scarcity is anchored in thermodynamic reality–its creation requires proof-of-work, ensuring that it remains rare. Meanwhile, its utility lies in offering a monetary alternative free from state and banking monopolies.

Finally, to understand utility, we can look to Zhuangzi, one of Taoism's foundational thinkers and author of one of the two foundational texts of Taoism. He tells of a twisted tree, which the carpenter cannot use, may grow undisturbed for a long time, while a straight tree will be cut into planks and sold by the lumberjack.

In this parable, uselessness guarantees longevity and life.

Similarly, imagine that you are in a small boat obstructing a large ship. You may be scolded by the ship's captain. But, if the small boat is unoccupied, the large ship will simply maneuver around it. In this example, the emptiness and uselessness of the small boat symbolize both its freedom, its ability to move within the "Way," and its submission to greater forces.

"The usefulness of what is depends on what is not."

— Tao Te Ching, verset 11

Bitcoin's utility lies in what it is not. It is not state-controlled, not reliant on trust, and not subject to arbitrary expansion. In contrast to a system that dictates the rules from above, Bitcoin operates as an open alternative, allowing individuals to opt out of a flawed system and participate in one where rules are enforced by mathematics rather than human discretion.

Part 3: Religion and Beliefs

17. Love

The influence of Romanticism redefined love at the dawn of the 19th century. Humans embarked on a quest for intense and ever-renewed sensations to drive the rampant consumption that the Industrial Revolution would soon require. Love became fuel for a system that thrives on desire, novelty, and perpetual dissatisfaction.

This modern, pagan vision of love, constantly reinforced by the entertainment industry, pulp novels, and mass-produced TV shows, stands in stark contrast to the Buddhist sense of love: "To love is to wish for the happiness of the other."

Wanting the happiness of another implies already knowing what brings them happiness, knowing them intimately and completely. This definition of love places the beloved and the lover in a quest as sublime as it is futile, for both, subject to the impermanence of being, constantly make and unmake this intimate knowledge.

To be in love is to take a few steps outside oneself and, thus, to feel larger. Yin seeks this emotional state because this unconscious longing facilitates a reduction of entropy through connection with others. Yang, on the other hand, prefers the capture and exchange of energy, especially sexual, or the reduction of entropy through knowledge of the environment. He does not overestimate the value of emotions.

If Yin surrenders herself to Yang, she expects to feel profound emotional fulfillment, to release her self-consciousness, and to surrender part of her independence to Yang. Yang understands that Yin must be selective. In return, Yin expects extreme happiness from experiencing positive emotions. These emotions arise from a reduction of entropy through the security and meaning that Yang brings to her daily life.

Today, Yin claims to be strong and independent when she feels that Yang is weak. But, deep within, Yin longs for this reduction of entropy through connection with a strong Yang, for this life, elevated to the point of dizziness, when Yin says she is in love. Simply said, when Yang appears weak, Yin will proclaim her independence, even as she longs for the intensity that love once promised.

Yang aspires to be loved without surrendering himself. He believes in love because he sees Yin in love, but he does not see himself as being in love. He fulfills himself through the feeling of possessing Yin, a possession that he knows deep down is fleeting.

In *Whatever*, Michel Houellebecq speaks of the difficulty of living and loving, of life being "out of reach" for some. In his thoroughly jubilant short novel about geeks, corporate life, and life in general, the author develops a theory of liberalism applied to the realm of sentiment, where this policy of love and sex creates the same extreme disparities found in economic wealth distributions.

The principle of conservation makes the capture of energy a zero-sum game. Just as capitalism produces winners and losers, so too does the sexual marketplace. Womanizers and incels, femme fatales and the forgotten. To love, one must love oneself and, therefore, manage one's own contradictions. Those who struggle with internal conflict often seek refuge in ideology – religious, political, or otherwise – as a way to silence the unbearable uncertainty of self-awareness. They experience it as an uncertainty that turns into narcissistic suffering.

Buddhist monk Ajahn Sujato observed, "If you don't like thinking, it's because you don't like a part of yourself." I am too aware of my own contradictions to ignore how detrimental it would be to stop thinking. Alain Finkielkraut wrote brilliantly about the defeat of thought on a societal level, but ideology (freezing thought) plays out just as destructively on an individual level.

Sex is more than an exchange of genetic information; it is also a sensory exchange. The brain is satisfied because it feels the intake of information through all the nerve endings in the skin. This intake reassures it of its ability to participate in reproduction.

Life, in its Darwinian cycle of death and renewal, is an expression of self-organization aimed at maximizing captured energy flow. The species benefits doubly from the process of reproduction, both through the multiplication of its members and the evolution of their capacities toward optimal adaptation.

This optimization has no meaning other than the maximization of energy. Energy has no anthropomorphic purpose, only scientific principles of operation. It is these principles that make the Anthropocene a natural phenomenon rather than a crushing reality for which we are guilty. Let us remember that science is a method for refuting existing knowledge, constantly verifying its alignment with a changing environment. In its approach, it is more a thermodynamic management of information than a social construct fantasized by non-scientists.

The duality between the feeling of belonging to the species (Yin - love - wave) and the search for existence as an individual lies at the heart of the Taoist representation of Yin and Yang. This interplay finds numerous parallels in physics, particularly in the wave-particle duality characteristic of light, which is both a wave and composed of photons. Yin symbolizes love and the wave, while Yang is mission and the photon.

This is why, as Peggy Sastre has accurately observed, Yin negotiates sex to obtain commitment (ensuring her relationship with her environment), while Yang negotiates commitment to obtain sex (fulfilling his mission through action).

When writing to his friend the cat about the consciousness of loving, Marcel Proust masterfully described what love can be for the animal, the embodiment of primordial innocence, and the polarity that opposes energies and brings beings together:

> *The indifference and boredom that tinted everything around me were dispelled since they were overshadowed by the white squirrel-cat that followed me everywhere, with the elegance of a king-bird and the sadness of a prophet. Dear, kind, silent creature, how you have kept me company during this life, which you have mysteriously and melancholically adorned.*

18. Happiness

Happiness reveals itself to us when reality, our aspirations, and our actions align.

It is not a fixed state but a dynamic that can fleetingly be detected in another through telling signs in circumstances that are unique to them. Making someone else happy, therefore, requires truly knowing them, and being happy requires truly knowing oneself.

For one person, happiness will be the future realization of a project; for another, it will be the fulfillment found in a sensory and immediately gratifying present; and for a third, it will be reconnecting with their roots. The greatest gift one can give to others is the expression of one's own happiness.

"You mustn't be afraid of happiness. It's just a good moment to experience."

– Romain Gary

Happiness is often confused today with well-being, when in fact, it is an unstable balance between detachment and direction on one hand and self-knowledge and connection with the rest of the living world on the other. This instability is the hallmark of life. A stable balance, according to the science of energy, is only found in a form of death, in immobility within a closed system, without interaction with the outside. Misunderstood well-being is the myth tied to this impossible-to-find equilibrium. In reality, happiness is the movement along the path, while well-being is a fleeting moment on that path.

Happiness is not a stock but the flow of decreasing entropy. This observation appears as early as the third verse of the Tao Te Ching (a transcription of Lao Tzu's thought from 2,500 years ago): "There is no path to happiness. Happiness is the path."

This understanding of happiness endures. In his letter to Simone Saintu on July 10, 1916, Louis Ferdinand Céline writes: "I selfishly enjoy the present moment - I believe it is the only formula for human happiness, the only one that doesn't deceive, the one we can truly rely on, since it depends on no one."

By reducing our focus to the present, we narrow our observed environment and thus reduce the uncertainty that comes with the expanse of our worries and our temporal horizon.

Beyond the reduction of entropy, another source of well-being nourishes us: the sensation of the flow of energy passing through us. Applied to money, it is not the stock of accumulated energy in the form of money, but the flow of energy entering and exiting that satisfies the dissipative structure that we are.

This is why money, as a representation of stored energy, does not bring happiness. Spending it does nothing to reduce the entropy of the compulsive buyer; it may even increase it through compulsive consumption. However, one can feel happiness at the news of a salary increase (incoming flow) or by making a donation (outgoing flow).

We feel pleasure when speeding down a slope, whether on a slide or a bike, through the transformation of gravitational potential energy into kinetic energy. These sensations of kinetic energy in motion reinforce our sense of being alive.

Happiness also manifests in the ability to desire, to know one's wants, and to have the will to obtain them. Humans obey the third principle both at the individual level and at the species level.

Humans tend to self-organize, not to stabilize but to maximize the flow of energy passing through them, using two different strategies that we can characterize as masculine (Yang) and feminine (Yin).

The reduction of entropy through connection with others is the essence of Yin. The aspiration to capture an increasing amount of energy is the essence of Yang. Modernity, however, presents a paradox. It brings us into a period where the energy capture of the species reaches such a level that it brings it closer to its inevitable extinction.

Extinction is a natural fluctuation of life, like any dissipative structure, as evidenced by the cycles of contraction and expansion on a cosmic scale, of which the Big Bang is a manifestation. When the production of entropy reaches its maximum, the structure dies out, gradually or abruptly.

When a plane goes into a spin, all the dials go haywire – a fitting metaphor for the destabilization of complex systems. The deconstruction of society began as early as the 1950s, paralleling the deconstruction of objects through the advent and rise of plastics, the defining material of productivism. Productivism corresponds to the acceleration of the energy flow captured by the species, a prelude to extinction.

The deconstruction of the Yin - Yang duality is a particularly anxiety - inducing stage of this process, a factor of division and a manifestation of a nihilistic ideology.

When the promotion of tolerance for a minority (homosexuals) is framed as necessitating increased suspicion toward the majority (heterosexuals) – as if they were opposing forces in a zero - sum equation – society does not gain equilibrium. Instead, collective happiness declines.

The creation of wealth consists of saving energy (reducing entropy - Yin) or releasing additional energy (exporting entropy - Yang). On an individual level, wealth corresponds to optionality, the freedom to choose among multiple possible states and life paths.

Henry David Thoreau described this freedom: "Wealth is the ability to fully experience life."

True wealth is having options – the freedom to navigate among different paths, to shape one's existence, rather than being constrained by circumstances. The pursuit of perfection is also an obstacle to happiness, as it makes achieving a result all the more uncertain by demanding perfection. According to Michel Houellebecq, "increasing desires to an unbearable level while making their fulfillment more and more inaccessible, this was the single principle upon which Western society rested."

Nietzsche argued that happiness is not a goal in itself but a byproduct of striving toward something greater. In praising slow and deep thinking, a process that reduces entropy, he said, "Whoever wishes to be lightning must remain a cloud for a long time."

A common misunderstanding surrounds the idea of "joyful sobriety." It is not a passive resignation to the world's problems—least of all climate change—but rather an acknowledgment of a fundamental principle governing life itself. There is no apathy in the face of climate change. Climate change is the expression of the third principle governing our deep functioning. We self-organize to maximize the flow of energy we capture, not to reduce it. The extinction of the species is not a fate to be avoided but a moment in the expansion-contraction cycle that characterizes dissipative structures. It is in light of this scientific reality that we must understand the message of renouncing the pursuit of sensations, as advocated by Buddhist philosophy. The Buddhist does not seek sensations but accepts them in order to experience them.

Moreover, Buddhism places more emphasis on reducing entropy through respect and knowledge of one's environment rather than through capturing additional energy. Unlike the Western impulse to control and reshape the world, Buddhist philosophy recognizes that it is neither our capacity nor our responsibility to understand or organize everything. Buddhists cooperate with their environment and adapt their participation according to their highest aspirations.

Engaging with risk can be a source of well-being when overcoming risk reduces uncertainty about the evolution of our observable universe, which, by definition, reduces entropy. In the same way, sports competition and the recognition of intellectual merit enhance the well-being of the group by organizing individuals' skills within the group, thus reducing the group's entropy.

Yin and Yang represent two paths to stability. Yin reduces entropy and increases well-being through connection, seeking stability in relationships, and group belonging. Yang seeks to reduce entropy through experience and knowledge, building order by mastering his environment.

The information Yang collects contributes to his self-organization, making him more capable of capturing a larger energy flow. Yin, however, seeks validation of her actions from others and fears solitude. Yang knows he is alone and attracts Yin because he projects toward Yin's confidence in his own reality. Yang is not desperate about being alone because he has integrated solitude into his understanding of the world around him. Yin is drawn to Yang's confidence in his identity. Yang builds his identity through his connection to reality, which is based on the acquisition of knowledge and the experience of action.

19. Confidence

Steve Jobs once said, "You don't trust tools. They are just tools; some work and some don't. But you do trust certain people."

Shared beliefs allow a large number of Homo sapiens to unite and form a society. Knowing that others share the same beliefs reduces each person's entropy and diminishes uncertainty about the other's behavior, thereby building mutual trust. Robert Axelrod's research on cooperation demonstrates how this social capital, in turn, catalyzes cooperation among the members of that society. Cooperation arises from trust, and trust emerges from the repetition of interactions, which characterizes a homogeneous and stable society.

The interactive guide *The Evolution of Trust*, inspired by Axelrod's *The Evolution of Cooperation* (1984) and its sequel, *The Complexity of Cooperation (2011)*, explores the ethics of reciprocity. Similarly, Robert Putnam's Bowling Alone highlights the decline of social capital in the United States, a warning about what happens when trust deteriorates.

Curiously, those who position themselves as the guarantors of trust and invoke it to justify their privileges – the so-called "trusted third parties" – are often the most selfish in defending their entitlements. In the game of trust, as in gambling, the one who knows the rules best is the most likely to exploit them. In reality, if a system becomes monopolistic through regulatory capture, mandatory use, and coercion, it is no longer based on trust.

Trust in the state, at least in theory, relates to its ability to manage resources and govern effectively. In practice, citizens increasingly doubt both the competence of governments and their ability to manage national wealth responsibly. Public trust in fiat money hinges on the proper functioning of payment networks and the illusion of controlled inflation, often minimized by skewed statistics.

What is fiat currency but a medium imposed by decree, one that central banks can create ex nihilo?

Consider France's public debt in 2022 reaching 3,000 billion euros, a figure that conveniently excludes civil servants' pensions, classified as "off-balance sheet" to obscure its full scale. Indeed, public accounting in Europe, unlike Anglo-Saxon countries, places civil servants' pensions "off-balance sheet," justifying this sleight of hand by claiming that the debt can be reduced by law! If we add this social debt, France's total public debt is actually close to 5,000 billion euros, almost twice the country's GDP.

Repaying such a debt can only be considered over a very long period. This implies an underlying assumption of the state's continued existence in its democratic form, which sustains citizens' trust in the state. An incompetent or incapable government is assumed to be replaceable.

The fallacy of this reasoning lies in the almost complete absence of incentives for fiscal responsibility. What government could seriously embark on a debt reduction project when the long-term benefits will never outweigh the short-term political drawbacks?

Only by raising interest rates on debt can the financial markets exert significant pressure. However, any government hiding behind the argument of interest rates ultimately sides with the usurers who orchestrate the exploitation of the middle class.

Interest rates on public debt are not merely financial tools; they are levers of control. They operate as tools to place a formerly sovereign country under the control of global finance via institutions like the International Monetary Fund (IMF), the European Union, or central banks.

It is these same institutions that drive politicians toward debt by creating the financial conditions for a race of electoral promises and clientelism. Politicians and governments, unable to restrain their spending, conveniently blame international treaties and financial institutions for their lack of autonomy while these institutions gradually assume supra-national governance over domestic economic policies. Monetary creation escapes the control of the state, which must turn to banks to finance itself at rates they set, perpetuating a cycle of crisis-driven central bank intervention and escalating debt. Who, then, can trust banks' management of the monetary system?

The real question is not how to restore trust in fiat currency but rather why people are denied the freedom to choose their currency in a system of open competition. To avoid this debate, central bankers disguise the supposed trust in their currency by conflating it with trust in the permanence of public authority.

20. Belief

What is proof?

One might naively think that it is what allows us to distinguish between belief and knowledge. Unfortunately, reality is more complex.

A belief can be based on proof, and proof requires a degree of belief.

For example, the equation $E = mc^2$ proves the equivalence between mass and energy. I can accept this equivalence either by believing in Einstein's work or by studying quantum physics to understand how he arrived at his equation.

In both cases, belief plays a role. Whether in the integrity of Einstein's work or in the reliability of the scientific method, proof is simply information that allows me to reduce my entropy. Entropy is a measure relative to an observer, which is why proof established by one experiment (by an observer) must be refutable by another experiment. This is also why science is a method for the systematic search for error.

Awareness of the relativity of entropy prevents us from falling into ideology, as brilliantly defined by Gérald Bronner, who noted, "Ideology is the unconditional expression of an idea that is only conditionally true."

In passing, we have linked belief and trust. By accepting the equation $E = mc^2$, I trust Einstein to have conducted his research and formulated an irrefutable conclusion, successfully tested by experiment.

A common belief can cement a group, but it is the absence of belief that defines the individual as something other than a member of the group.

As the biologist-philosopher Thomas Durand rightly observed, the word belief has become so polysemic that it can now apply to any mental representation. Thus, we are witnessing a kind of negation of skepticism through an injunction to believe rather than to doubt.

This is how atheists are mistakenly labeled as believers, as if rejecting the existence of God were a form of faith. Yet the absence of proof is not proof of absence. It is possible that, in an indeterminate future, proof of non-existence may emerge, but for now, atheists simply do not believe in his existence.

God is a concept, but a particular kind of concept – a predatory one. He is capable of killing any other concept that crosses his path, starting with that of proof. According to believers, the absence of proof of God's existence and the multiple contradictions in the scriptures are explained by the very concept of God. By this logic, God is both the generator and the destroyer of proof. The notion of refutable proof does not need to be debated because long before, the concept of proof was carried off on a stretcher.

Moreover, one must acknowledge that believers possess a certain talent for inventing parables. This one, reported by Wayne Dyer in his book *The Sacred Self*, is particularly poetic. Two babies in the womb are having a conversation.

> One asks the other: "Do you believe in life after birth?"
>
> The other replies: "Of course. There must be something after birth. Maybe we're only here to prepare ourselves for what's to come after."
>
> "That's absurd," says the first. "There's no life after birth. What kind of life would that be?"
>
> The second responds: "I don't know, but there will probably be more light than here. Maybe we'll be able to walk with our legs and eat with our mouths. Maybe we'll experience new sensations, unimaginable now?"
>
> The first retorts: "That makes no sense: walking is impossible, and eating with our mouths is ridiculous. The umbilical cord provides everything we need. Life after birth is ruled out by logic."

> The second insists: "I think there's something after birth, and it might be different from here. Maybe we won't need the umbilical cord anymore."
>
> The first responds: "If there's life after birth, why has no one ever come back from it? Birth is the end of life, and after birth, there's only darkness, silence, and oblivion."
>
> "I don't know," says the second, "but we will surely meet our mother, and she will take care of us."
>
> The first replies: "Our mother? Do you really believe in the existence of our mother? That's ridiculous. If our mother exists, where is she?"
>
> The second says: "She's all around us. We live thanks to her and in her. Without her, this world wouldn't exist."
>
> The first baby says: "But I don't see her."
>
> The second concludes: "Sometimes, in the silence, when you focus and listen, you can sense her presence and hear her loving voice speaking to you from above."

The intended moral is clear: just as a fetus cannot comprehend its mother's existence, humans cannot grasp God's, but that does not mean he isn't there. The story is intriguing, but it is not proof. It functions as a belief amplifier and reinforces faith without evidence.

Belief is not fed by proof, but rather, it loves fables. The fable of the hare and the tortoise illustrates the difference between an exception and a trend. Even though hares tend, statistically, to be faster, you can always find one that will be overtaken in a race by a tortoise. Based on this, we are told that if hares outperform in a fair race, we must turn it into a handicap race so that tortoises have the same chances as the hares.

In 2023, I received an email from the Foundation of the École Polytechnique, which stated:

> *Diversifying the recruitment of students in the Polytechnician program is a major challenge for*

> *the École Polytechnique, and more broadly for selective French programs. The overrepresentation of boys, students from the Île-de-France region, and the most privileged social categories remains too pronounced.*

The denunciation of alleged favoritism replaces the recognition of merit. A fair race, an opportunity for social mobility and a path to excellence, is thus disappearing in favor of a handicap race.

The belief in the dominance of nurture has erased the evidence of the determinism of nature, an insistence that all disparities in achievement are due to systemic barriers rather than inherent differences. Yin and Yang are confused and presumed interchangeable.

21. The Intangible

From Einstein and his famous equation, we know that matter is a form of energy. Mass is equivalent to energy. Each body has mass energy, even when at rest. This mass energy can be released by mobilizing an activation energy, which varies depending on the body in question.

In its most diffused form, energy can condense into elementary particles, which then self-organize into atoms and eventually into matter. Matter then self-organizes into stars and planets, some of which are populated by living species. In fact, according to the third principle, all these systems, from elementary particles to the entire universe, are dissipative structures that self-organize to maximize the energy flow they can capture.

Atoms are mostly composed of empty space. To grasp this, consider that the electron orbiting the nucleus is the size of a fly in your living room. Your living room represents the space where the fly-electron has a probability of being found.

Therefore, when your hand, composed of molecules, holds a gold coin, it isn't really touching it. The gold coin is actually levitating in the palm of your hand. A tough truth for those who believe they can distinguish the tangible from the intangible, the real from the "virtual."

The void corresponds to a local absence of energy. Energy is not there but can return as it contracts and expands. Absence is defined as a very low or null probability of presence. The void is merely probabilistic and remains elusive.

Heisenberg's inequalities, known as the uncertainty principle, are a direct consequence of wave - particle duality. One of these inequalities implies that it is possible to borrow energy from the vacuum for a very short time. Later, in 1948, the Casimir effect introduced the concept of vacuum energy – the idea that even "empty" space possesses energy. If the vacuum has a defined energy without an additive constant, it could behave as if it has mass. Energy exists only with a probability density, and the vacuum corresponds to an infinitely low probability. A dissipative structure – whether a star, a human body, or a cryptocurrency network – acts as the mechanism that organizes this energy, preventing it from dispersing completely into entropy. The vacuum itself is not truly empty. It gives birth to matter and antimatter, which, when they meet, unite to create light and emptiness. Creation and destruction are two sides of the same process. In this framework, the line between existence and nonexistence, the tangible and the intangible, dissolves, showing that what many call "real" is an interlinked core of energy, probability, and perception.

22. Religion

To return to the dharma expressed in this book, we can say that energy appears as the ultimate force governing the universe.

Understanding how energy works provides a more fruitful and objective key to interpreting natural and social phenomena than adopting any particular religious belief. This understanding does not, of course, prevent one from believing in a god, but it reduces his intervention to the establishment of physical principles, effectively replacing the role of a divine creator with that of an inventor.

The naïve hope for eternal life gives way to the wonder of the present through the discernment of beauty. To reduce his entropy, Yang leans toward skepticism, seeking refutation, while Yin takes refuge in belief, a guarantee of belonging to a protective group.

Believers and skeptics are two recurring characters in the human comedy, constantly coexisting within each of us in our thoughts and actions. Secularism allows for the peaceful coexistence of belief with skepticism.

However, from one individual to another, while both tendencies may express themselves, their speaking time varies dramatically depending on the topic. The complexity of human nature means that we find mystical scientists and religious people passionate about astrophysics.

Public adherence to a belief signifies connection with a group. Believers exercise their skepticism selectively, primarily on ideas that might challenge their faith.

Group affiliation has been one of the driving forces behind *Sapiens'* conquest of the world, both for collective action and protection from individuals outside the group and predators within it. Our desire to belong to a group influences our social behaviors and encourages us to maneuver rather than directly criticize group thinking.

Basing one's opinions on facts derived from a changing reality goes against the stability and trust sought in an ally. The realist's ideas adjust according to their experiences rather than their allegiances. Every group generates its own *doxa*, a common belief that cements its identity.

Skeptics, on the other hand, prefer to seek proof of a statement before accepting it. They rely on belief only for the knowledge that remains inaccessible to them. They aim to limit this part of belief to the bare minimum. They are the minority, the heretics, the rebels, and the dissidents, in Salman Rushdie's terms, who push society forward toward ever-greater energy capture, mistakenly called progress, when it is in fact merely the expression of the third principle.

A monetary system reflects these two facets: belief and skepticism. Money has a use value, dependent on its recognition by the group (social trust, based on a common belief in its value, sometimes imposed by law in a monopoly) and a value backed by its energy counterpart, which must be verifiable by skeptics.

$$V = S + E$$

This equation reflects a thesis of this book, namely that for a monetary system, the value of money results from its social value (S) and its energy value (E).

V: Value of the monetary system.
S: Social value of the monetary system, which is a function of the energy saved and released compared to a barter economy. The energy saved corresponds to the reduction of movement in space of exchanged goods (we eliminate the need for the coincidence of wants in the same place).

The energy released corresponds to goods and services exchanged at different times (we also eliminate the need for the coincidence of wants in time).

This represents the energy (saved or released) associated with goods and services that could not have been exchanged in a barter economy.

S is a function of the size of the acceptance network. It primarily satisfies believers and can be defined as a use value or social credit.

E: Energy value, the counterpart to the issuance of the currency in question. It determines the scarcity of the currency and reassures skeptics by limiting monetary creation.

More precisely, the energy counterpart complements the social use value. The social value expresses the *Yin* energy of money, while the energy value represents its *Yang* aspect. This duality strengthens rather than weakens the monetary system, as it focuses on the two axes of value – one directed towards believers, the other towards skeptics.

For fiat money, the energy counterpart is provided by borrowers who promise to devote a portion of their work to repayments. Unfortunately, skeptics cannot verify in real time whether the increase in the money supply corresponds to solvable promises. The centralized nature of fiat, which promotes opacity, along with the multitude of projects and individuals being financed, makes any verification illusory, if not impossible.

Belief in fiat money is therefore sustained by monopoly. Its use value is inflated by forced usage, while the energy value is manipulated through an opaque and discretionary monetary creation mechanism controlled by an oligarchy.

In contrast, Bitcoin's energy counterpart is easily verifiable through the difficulty of mining. Although the precise amount of energy monetized by miners can only be estimated due to the heterogeneous nature of equipment and locations, the system itself remains open to scrutiny. Its social use value is more elusive because of its purely optional nature and competition with all other currencies.

This structure suggests a monetary version of secularism: the separation of money and state, just as religious secularism separates church from state. Religious secularism prevents religious institutions from holding political power, particularly in education.

In this definition, the word "church" refers to institutions revolving around a religion, mainly the regular and secular clergy or associations, with a religion being a set of beliefs that delineates a "sacred" realm from a so-called "profane" domain. The sacred represents a fixed truth, impermeable to criticism, in contrast to scientific truth.

The definition of secularism by Islamists and their collaborators slightly deviates from the dictionary and could be stated as: "An Islamophobic approach, disguised as republican ideals, aimed at discriminating against Muslims by preventing them from practicing their faith freely." Thus, we have a fine example of an anti-concept. Religion teaches doing good, but secularism questions a religious definition of good, instead advocating resistance to evil.

Philippe Silberzahn summarizes this dialectic, which spans centuries of philosophical thought from Machiavelli to Hannah Arendt, passing through Karl Popper: "Evil is tangible; it is the current reality, easily identifiable."

Good is intangible; it is a hoped-for future in the name of which one may commit all manner of crimes because, while the ends are hypothetical, the means employed are always tangible because they are present.

For those who pursue good, the means matter little. Doing good often ends with the saying, "You can't make an omelet without breaking eggs," to which Orwell quipped: "I've seen the broken eggs, but where's the omelet?"

Michel Houellebecq aptly notes that, for any given individual, not all religions are equal. For him, what allows one to judge the value of a religion is the quality of the morality it enables.

In contrast to Nietzsche and his refutation of morality and pity, Houellebecq sees a "moral absolute" independent of religions and superior to them. Like Pascal, he believes that religion "offers the feeling of not being a stranger in an indifferent world."

This is one of the problems with religion. It fills a void, imposing itself most easily on those who feel lost or ignorant.

Only the teachings of Buddha present a perspective different from the religions of the Book, recognizing in all beings a capacity to connect and function in a network, in a prosaic rather than metaphysical sense, through compassion. Schopenhauer's philosophy seeks the same state of grace through contemplation.

Auguste Comte, the founder of positivism, even attempted to lay the foundations of a future religion compatible with scientific progress. It is no coincidence that religious discourse often shares the embellished qualities of poetry, as Michel Houellebecq emphasizes: "It's an absolute discourse that aims to assert statements without the possibility of negation."

Secularism and Freedom of Expression

"It is easier to make defenders of secularism look outdated than to confront Islamists. Opening a discussion on secularism rather than on Islamism is already a form of cowardice."

– Riss (Charlie Hebdo, 6/3/19)

Secularism is not just policy; it is a safeguard that allows the existence of a community beyond religion, such as the national community. Each citizen is then recognized first as an individual, not as a believer or non-believer. Religion is thus reduced to the status of an opinion based on belief. Unlike opinions formed from verifiable facts, it reveals its irrational nature and becomes open to criticism.

More broadly, secularism considers non-believers, atheists, and agnostics to be as rational, sensitive, and respectable as believers.

If a religion is a mythological belief based on an ancient ideological corpus that produces opinions on everything and anything, these opinions cannot claim a sacred character that exists only in the circular logic of the believer.

Against the intimidation of the clergy and the terror of fanatics, secularism defends the right to criticize them and refutes the very notion of blasphemy. Blasphemy is a religious concept that forbids free criticism of religion by treating it as a crime, exactly like a dictator does with opposition. The qualification of criticism as blasphemy falls strictly under the religious domain and is accompanied by condemnation, creating an obvious asymmetry of risk. There is almost no risk for the religious party, while the critic faces the maximum risk (death).

Without secularism, there is no freedom of expression, as any religion could condemn any opinion. After all, religion is just an opinion that decides to label another opinion as blasphemy.

For example, blasphemy was only decriminalized in Italy in 1999, and it remains an administrative offense. Through terror, Islamists also create an asymmetry of perception between the overestimated risk of speaking out in the short term and the underestimated risk of staying silent in the longer term.

Furthermore, in the face of adversity, denial of reality allows an escape from sterile thinking that is incapable of finding a solution. The expression of denial plays a role in constructing this refuge, which explains why people in denial often appear deeply convinced.

Freedom of Conscience Versus Theocracy

Secularism stands as an obstacle to the instrumentalization of religion for political purposes. It affirms freedom of conscience as individual sovereignty in the spiritual realm, rejecting groupthink that would be imposed by a religion. Non-believers or secular believers exist as thinking beings who are ready to express themselves and are resistant to adopting ready-made thinking.

Some people identify their civilization with a religion, assuming it to be its foundation. This is why, even without overt radical convictions or being unaware of the radicality of their stance, they find it difficult to accept secularism.

To better disqualify and render it unintelligible or even inapplicable, they label secularism as "inclusive" or "open," twisting its meaning to create loopholes for intolerance and proselytism. They disguise it as ecumenism while considering other religions as heresies, atheism as a pathology, and apostasy as a crime. Islamists also coined the term "Islamophobia," which they later associate with secularism, a concept they despise, in order to discredit any critique. In doing so, they reverse the consequence of terror – *Islamophobia*, meaning, etymologically, the fear of Islam – into its cause or even justification.

Their ideology divides the world into believers and "heedless" individuals, the latter reduced to the rank of cattle, as stated in verse 179 of Surah 7 in the Quran:

> *We have created for Hell many of the jinn and humankind. They have hearts with which they do not understand, eyes with which they do not see, and ears with which they do not hear. They are like cattle – no, even more astray. These are the heedless.*

Secularism, however, seeks to erase this division in the public sphere, limiting its impact on the private circle.

A Fragile Democratic Process

Secularism is not a luxury of civilization but one of its foundations. A civilized person has internalized social constraints and accepted that others may not believe or think as they do.

Secularism is not a final achievement but a political process aimed at separating religion from the state to prevent it from taking control. Fundamentalism and infiltration can easily disrupt this process, highlighting the fragility of individual sovereignty in the face of religion.

One of the most insidious threats to secularism comes from ideological infiltration. In Islam, the practice of dissimulation (*taqiyya*) is directly embedded in the doctrine, allowing followers to conceal their beliefs when necessary. This, combined with the globalization of extremes, enables the gradual imposition of totalitarian religious views on democracies paralyzed by "human-rights-ism."

The Tolerance Paradox

Finally, fundamentalists, whether skillfully or unconsciously projecting their extremism onto their opponents, accuse them of intolerance, conveniently ignoring the paradox of tolerance. Tolerance cannot tolerate intolerance. Thomas Mann warned of this in *The Magic Mountain*: "Tolerance becomes a crime when it applies to evil." Plato described the necessity of a "benevolent despotism," a concept Karl Popper later developed in *The Open Society and Its Enemies*.

In other words, intolerance cannot be confused with resistance to the intolerable. The symbolic figure of the King of the United Kingdom, head of the Anglican Church, acts as a benevolent despot within the Commonwealth. The ceremony surrounding the royal family relegates other religions to the status of guests. There are prayers in Parliament and reserved seats for clergy in the House of Lords. In France, where the civil code stipulates assimilation as a condition for citizenship (see Articles 21-24), the process of secularism remains the last bastion against separatism and theocratic infiltration.

Secularism must be actively defended against those who seek to erode it. Marylin Maeso captured the danger well:

> *Each time we treat as condemnable provocateurs those who have only ever sought to provoke thought, we empower those who are willing to do anything to extinguish thinking.*

23. Science

Science: "A coherent body of knowledge relating to certain categories of facts, objects, or phenomena that follow laws and/or are verified by experimental methods. Each of the branches of knowledge or learning (often plural): Mathematical sciences."

Science is a method for questioning existing knowledge and thus accumulating verifiable knowledge. It is not an encyclopedia, the sum of knowledge at any given moment.

When Descartes wrote, "I think, therefore I am," he meant that we can tell ourselves stories about almost anything and deceive ourselves about almost everything except the act of doubting.

We tell ourselves stories to belong to a group, but to truly exist as individuals, we must embrace doubt. Science is the method of doubt, and doubt is a way of thinking. It allows us to stop deceiving ourselves and start existing.

Individual existence is the true purpose of science because, without it, there are only groups, clans, and the species.

There is a thermodynamic asymmetry between falsehood and truth. It costs nothing to utter a lie (creationists), but refuting it with verifiable evidence (Darwin) requires significant effort. Relativism exacerbates the effects of this asymmetry. Brandolini's law states that the amount of energy needed to refute nonsense is much greater than that required to produce it.

The statement of a proposition only raises the question of its truthfulness. Only the demonstration that confirms or invalidates the proposition contributes new information, thus reducing entropy—i.e., a flow of energy.

Epistemology (from the ancient Greek **ἐπιστήμη** / *epistémê* "true knowledge, science" and **λόγος** / *lógos* "discourse") refers to the critical study of science and scientific knowledge. But, epistemology has been hijacked by relativism, a pillar of modern woke ideology, which rejects objective truth and reduces everything to subjective interpretation. Relativism, one of the foundational elements of woke ideology, is a deviation from epistemology that claims all truth, and consequently the pursuit of truth, is subjective. In a relativist (woke) context, one wins a debate by shouting louder than others and silencing the opposition.

Relativism fosters confusion among the virtual, intangible, and real. Energy is intangible, yet no one disputes that its effects are very real. Information is equivalent to energy, yet the media frequently use the word "virtual" to describe the digital economy or decentralized digital currencies. However, when discussing central bank digital currencies, they are careful not to label them as virtual.

Among the many topics that epistemology has examined, the unity of science is essential, identifying four pillars: formal sciences (mathematics, mathematical logic), exact sciences (physics, chemistry, engineering sciences), life sciences, and social sciences and humanities. However, the latter category has been increasingly infiltrated by thinkers without scientific training and is now overrepresented. Astrophysicist François Roddier, drawing on the works of Per Bak and Ilya Prigogine, has emphasized that thermodynamics, particularly the third law, offers a key to understanding human behavior.

This third law, also known as the principle of maximization of entropy production (MEP), states that any open system self-organizes to maximize the flow of energy through it. Simply put, every living being integrates information about its environment to capture as much energy as possible. This law is consistently verified with remarkable fractal coherence, regardless of the scale of observation, from the infinitely small to the infinitely large, from atoms to the observable universe, and from individuals to entire species.

In the real world, every system is open in terms of energy. A closed system exists only in a laboratory or as a thought experiment. Understanding this third law, Ilya Prigogine used the term "dissipative structure" to describe an open system.

Fluctuations (cycles of births and extinctions) are intrinsic to this principle of self-organization. Without them, energy would cease to self-organize into such a diversity of forms.

There are different, non-exclusive strategies to maximize the conversion (capture and dissipation) of energy: alignment (crystals, magnetism), growth (bodies, populations), enhancement of physical abilities, and enhancement of cognitive abilities. Alignment and cognitive abilities help reduce entropy, while growth and physical abilities allow the capture of a larger energy flow. In summary, self-organization results in a concomitant increase in the amount of energy captured and the capacity to capture it.

Some believers seek to find an explanation for science and claim that scientific evidence doesn't prove science. They project their worldview onto an idea that disturbs them, while science is simply a method and claims nothing more. It proves its strength in practical applications and replicable experiments. The problem for zealots is that, since Galileo and Darwin, science has continuously provided more evidence that disproves their mythological narratives. The "need for illusion" mentioned by Saul Bellow seems insatiable. Yet, the more knowledge progresses, the further magical thinking must distance itself from rationality to persist.

Rationality is not the same as intelligence. Indeed, rationality is intelligence applied to the search for solutions to real problems. Intelligence has evolved more as a tool for seeking well-being, belonging to a group, social status, and sex than as a tool for seeking objective truth. Group loyalty often conflicts with objective truth because truth is not always pleasant, especially when it challenges the interests of those in power. This phenomenon, known as motivated reasoning, occurs when we use our intelligence and experience in the service of irrational goals. Curiosity remains the best remedy against prejudice, and humility is essential for questioning one's own beliefs.

The main issue with religious doctrines is not the hypothesis of the existence of a god but that of the immortality of the soul. From an atheist's perspective, the mind is inseparable from the body and does not survive it. The soul would thus be an ideological construct that denies the impermanence of the mind, which changes and ages like the organism to which it belongs.

Buddhism avoids this hypothesis of immortality by acknowledging the impermanence of all things, including the soul, and the cyclical nature of all existence, in a succession of life and death, of expansion and contraction of entropy.

Scientifically, if time has neither beginning nor end, this cycle of perpetual rebirth makes sense. Indeed, the minuscule probability that the atoms constituting an individual would recombine to bring them back to life exactly as before becomes a certainty over an infinite number of random draws. However, the human mind did not evolve to grasp the concept of infinity easily.

The Big Bang Theory is sometimes used to support the supposed necessity of a "creator." The argument goes as follows: According to the second law of thermodynamics, a closed system spontaneously evolves towards its maximum entropy. If our observable universe were a system isolated from external influences, it should then be heading towards its thermodynamic death – a state where nothing moves, with atoms sufficiently dispersed to no longer interact with each other.

The proof of the existence of a creator would be in the fact that our universe has a beginning and an end date. An infinitely ancient and eternal universe is less compatible with this belief. No beginning, no creator! The absence of an end of the world also contradicts religious texts.

But this is a misunderstanding. Our observable universe is expanding and, therefore, is not an isolated system. The second law does not apply to it because open systems receive energy that can reduce their entropy. They are governed by the third law (MEP).

Our observable universe will therefore self-organize to maximize the flow of energy through it, just as grains of sand self-organize into a pile. Just as the height of the sandpile oscillates around a critical value when a continuous flow of sand is poured, the observable universe will be subject to quantum fluctuations, with phases of expansion followed by contractions – the Big Bang itself likely resulting from such a fluctuation.

In any case, the idea that our observable universe will have an end is not proven. If time has neither a beginning nor an end, it is statistically possible that our atoms could one day recombine to reform the same person in a time very far from now, almost infinite on our timescale. Similarly, it is certain that if you roll two dice an unlimited number of times, you will inevitably roll double sixes.

At the microscopic level, quantum physics has proven that the future can influence the past, which challenges our perception of time flowing in only one direction. The transition to the macroscopic scale produces artifacts resulting from the second law (the entropy of an isolated system can only increase), such as the sensation of time's passage or consciousness—that is, the interference between the past self and the present self. The only thing that truly exists is energy, which self-organizes according to the third law (MEP) into various forms, such as matter ($E = mc^2$), the observable universe, animal and plant species, and more.

Energy was not created since it emerges from interactions between matter and antimatter or, by definition, from the vacuum. Cosmology is indeed at the frontier of science.

In *The Logic of Scientific Discovery* (1934), Austrian philosopher of science Karl Popper defines a theory as scientific if it is refutable and can be supported or disproved by experiments. He even writes that the more refutable it is, the more scientific it is. In other words, "the more a theory is compatible with a diversity of empirical results, the less likely it is to be refuted, and thus the less scientific it is."

"The vulnerability through exposure to observations is the primary goal of any theory."

– Hermann Bondi

Science is a method aimed at defining a truth objectified through experience. The whistleblower engages in politics of truth motivated by ethics, adhering to the "force of the true," with truth being defined as that which withstands the test of real experience. According to Michel Foucault, *parrhesiasts* (like Plato) undertake to speak the truth at an indeterminate price, which can extend to their own death. In any case, merely contesting the *doxa* or the result of "group thinking" is rarely rewarded.

Yuval Harari notes that religion responds to the need for order, while science is more focused on power (the power to heal, to travel, etc.). But one can also state the inverse. Religion seeks power over people, while science gives people power over their environment, even though these powers converge. Science also responds to the need for order by explaining natural phenomena. It is a method for reducing humanity's entropy, thereby reducing humanity's uncertainty about the evolution of its observable environment.

In the so-called experimental sciences, knowledge is built or dismantled through experimentation, whereas, in mathematics, it is constructed on axioms, particularly Peano's axioms for arithmetic and Euclid's axioms for geometry.

Gödel's two incompleteness theorems are often misinterpreted to cast doubt on science, though their implications are far more nuanced. His first incompleteness theorem states that a system of axioms cannot be both complete (if something is true, it is provable) and consistent (one cannot prove both a statement and its opposite).

Gödel's second incompleteness theorem extends this idea and tells us that the consistency of a system of axioms cannot be proven from within the system itself, echoing the second law of thermodynamics.

In other words, mathematical knowledge cannot be reduced to a finite set of axioms. Similarly, we cannot prove that mathematics is free of contradictions. Just as our knowledge of the real world is contingent on experience, mathematics contains an element of uncertainty about what is provable or a degree of inconsistency in what is proven.

Science, as a method, encounters a great challenge in probing the nature of the vacuum – an enigma more elusive than tangible reality. If energy is everything and everywhere, the vacuum is simply the absence of energy, understood in a probabilistic rather than deterministic sense. The vacuum is the near - certainty of the absence of energy.

Another way to "see the vacuum" scientifically is to think of it as resulting from the coexistence or collision between particles and antiparticles (the collision between an electron and a positron results in the disappearance of both particles, emitting light), between matter and antimatter, and between visible energy and dark energy. The vacuum, then, is not an inert nothingness but a battleground of fleeting presences and absences – a paradox woven into the very fabric of the universe.

Part 4: Society and Liberties

24. Conspiracy

Conspiracy: "Harm to the fundamental interests of the nation. A coordinated resolution to commit an attack materialized by one or more acts. By extension, a more or less reprehensible plan for an action carried out collectively and secretly."

Some people struggle with the truth when it doesn't align with their ideas – a tendency we all share to some degree, though some find reality particularly challenging. Recently, a journalist on a news channel lamented that a collective was sharing videos on insecurity, urban violence, and miscellaneous incidents. His complaint? That the group was "far-right." For this self-righteous journalist, the character of those speaking became more important than the truth itself.

This is the signature of the ideologue: he doesn't listen to the expression of a new idea to understand it but to respond with his own idea. Everyone is, therefore, ready to talk about conspiracy. The publication of Bitcoin's invention under a pseudonym (Satoshi Nakamoto) would then supposedly be part of a conspiracy aimed at challenging the monopoly of money creation. Let's first note that denial preceded the accusations of conspiracy. Banking lobbyists claim that Bitcoin is not a currency because it is too volatile. It's not a "stablecoin," meaning a currency whose value is pegged to a state currency. It is an energy standard in the form of secure, divisible, and transferable tokens, and thus a monetary standard.

Given the weakness of their arguments, other defenders of the status quo have labeled Bitcoiners as conspiracists on the grounds that they criticize a banking oligarchy that benefits from the monopoly of money creation. Yet, in a neutral definition, a conspiracist denounces a conspiracy, whether supposed or real.

We are thus witnessing a reversal of meaning, where the conspirator, who supports the conspiracy of cryptocurrencies aimed at abolishing the monopoly, becomes a conspiracist, just as a victim would become a culprit.

The increasing confusion of terms is merely a symptom of an ideology that is becoming more prevalent. Absurd thinking becomes a badge of group membership, and mechanically, rationality that challenges absurd thinking becomes a threat to this group. According to artificial intelligence researcher Eliezer Yudkowsky, you measure your rationality by the gap between your confusion about fiction and your confusion about reality.

Ideology, like any belief, is born from the desire to belong to a group. It sometimes opposes reality when reality contradicts the ideology. Rather than compromise their status as a group member, the ideologue prefers to deny reality itself. Lacking substantive arguments, they dismiss contradiction with indignation, invoking offense like a child whose toy has been broken. To strike back, the ideologue attaches the suffix -phobia (homophobia, Islamophobia, fatphobia) to any criticism, to any non-conforming thought, labeling it as a neurosis to justify censorship.

"It is important that people with very little sense of humor (due to their lack of understanding of the importance of context) do not have the power to censor works that are appreciated by those who understand the significance of context."

– John Cleese, founding member of Monty Python

In general, the accusation of conspiracy theory is thrown around as soon as someone dares to criticize a system of power or make connections between seemingly unrelated topics. Such accusations typically come from the "managers" and are directed at the "innovators." This second point–the ability to connect distinct subjects ("connecting the dots") to find a solution–is the hallmark of innovators, as Steve Jobs highlighted in his famous 2005 commencement speech at Stanford University.

Unlike management, innovation involves not censoring bad ideas but embracing them as necessary steps toward achieving the best ones. Our brain identifies them as bad, which helps it gradually define, either intuitively or rationally, what will later be considered better ideas and how to produce them. The creative process begins with imitation, followed by recognizing why the imitation is inferior, and then reiterating in imitation until something original is found. Managers often excel at thorough analysis but rarely match innovators in creative solution - finding. See, Karl Marx. Whereas innovators often rely on a quick analysis of the existing situation, focusing on the essentials. See Steve Jobs, who recounted how, after being fired by Apple's managers, the burden of success was replaced by the freedom of starting anew.

The power system, generally seen as benevolent and virtuous by managers, is often viewed as corrupt by innovators. Grant power to any group without a counterbalance, and abuse eventually follows.

For supporters of the status quo, the notion of conspiracy theory allows them to pathologize their opponents, suggesting that they suffer from paranoia. The logical extension would be confinement in asylums – a step Stalin took readily with his gulag system. In a lighter version, the conspiracy theory is wielded as a naive image of a counterpower, which can then be discredited to maintain the status quo. According to Wikipedia:

> *A conspiracy theory is a type of discourse that describes an event as primarily resulting from the planned and concealed actions of a group, different from the apparent actors, while disregarding the historical investigative approach (multi-causal and open to hypotheses) in favor of a perspective that sees signs of this group's intervention and power everywhere, even in the fact that evidence is lacking (which would be proof of the conspirators' concealment power).*

In the case of the monetary monopoly, the "group" is quite large, as it includes all the beneficiaries of the monopoly. The beneficiaries are numerous and include central bankers, commercial bankers who create money by issuing credit, and the main borrowers themselves (governments, large corporations, wealthy individuals). The only losers are the environment (exploited by the financing of harmful projects) and the masses of ordinary individuals reduced to servitude by the major beneficiaries of money creation.

The monetary monopoly has transitioned from being a conspiracy to a state conspiracy, an institution. Thus, we can no longer even speak of a conspiracy. It has become entrenched in law through the monetary and financial code, with no democratic process to challenge it. An unassailable institution, like the central bank, is the hallmark of a successful conspiracy and the failure of democracy.

The industrial counterpart of conspiracy is machination. When we replace humans with machines, we mobilize a stock of energy (the machine), whereas hiring a worker ensures a flow of energy (their labor). Acquiring a stock of energy requires access to a stock of money, while hiring a worker only involves a flow.

Since the machine is more powerful than the human it replaces, we talk about productivity gains, and the one who buys the machine widens the gap with the one who hires a human. The machine has no will, but the desire of managers for replacement leads to the robotization of life. The little gray men want a gray and risk-free life for everyone, just like themselves. *Tiny Lives*, to borrow a title from Pierre Michon.

Those who, through society's machinations, are freed from any manual labor have acquired the privilege of denying reality at the cost of dispossessing those who actually work. Yet, some want us to believe that misinformation is more dangerous than censorship or that criticizing an institution is more dangerous than the institution itself – a final inversion that reveals how thoroughly the conspiratorial mindset has captured those who claim to stand against it.

25. Equality

Equality: "The absence of any discrimination between human beings in terms of their rights: political, civil, and social equality."

"There is indeed a vigorous and legitimate passion for equality that drives men to want to be strong and respected. This passion tends to elevate the small to the rank of the great; but there is also, in the human heart, a depraved taste for equality, which leads the weak to want to bring the strong down to their level, reducing men to prefer equality in servitude over inequality in freedom."

– Alexis de Tocqueville (1805-1859), *Democracy in America*

Let us first note that, since rights are associated with duties, a complete definition of equality should also encompass any discrimination regarding duties.

Is employment discrimination anything more than an employer's discernment – their concern for team cohesion and quality while operating under the harsh laws of competition? Can the freedom to undertake be protected against the excesses of an out-of-control administration without safeguards? The entrepreneur may feel that some moral guardians want to interfere with their choices without bearing the slightest responsibility for the outcomes.

An egalitarian vision presupposes that employees are interchangeable, despite the daily evidence showing that the success of a team depends on its members. This form of egalitarianism effectively strips employees of responsibility for outcomes and, therefore, for their work.

Non-discrimination also pertains to a planned economy, where the collective relies on the law of an oligarchy to legislate on crucial aspects of exchange. For example, one might begin by interfering with the hiring process and continue, perhaps, with the price-setting mechanism. In the USSR, most prices were set by Moscow, creating conditions for shortages.

Egalitarians aim to separate cultural criteria from skills or experience, but no employer needs them to determine when a candidate's strengths outweigh their supposed weaknesses. An employer searching for talent is, by definition, aware of its rarity and eager to find it. Recruitment is a challenging exercise with high costs for the employer, where uncertainty cannot be easily resolved, even after a trial period.

Feminists demand gender parity in political power positions (while already holding a majority in corporate roles, particularly in HR and communications), yet curiously, they do not demand parity in the difficult and dangerous jobs in construction, industry, and security, domains where men are overwhelmingly represented – just as they are among the homeless.

This selective aspiration for gender parity can only stem from an ideology that denies the polarity between feminine and masculine essences, the polarity that gives rise to a desire for what one cannot possess.

It's worth noting that sexual reproduction is also a consequence of the third principle of thermodynamics. Self-organizing evolution is accelerated both in energy capture (one sex focuses on reproduction while the other can devote more energy to resource acquisition) and in genetic mixing (self-organization of the species).

By conflating discrimination with discernment, Wokeism seeks to erase the polarity between feminine and masculine, between Yin and Yang, which is essential for establishing an energy flow between two beings, much like the magnetic attraction between metal and a magnet.

When we don't understand how a computer system works, we tend to confuse bugs with features. Similarly, by ignoring the third principle, woke ideology seeks to erase the differences between the sexes without realizing that this is a feature of society, not a bug to be fixed. The predominantly Yang man thrives with competition, while the woman often excels in cooperation when expressing her predominance of Yin.

Regarding Yang's greater aptitude for competition, experiments and statistics prove conclusive. Among the world's top 100 chess players, only one is female, despite widespread encouragement for girls to play chess across Western nations. In less cerebral sports, the differences are even more pronounced: the French women's 100-meter record (10.76 seconds) barely surpasses that of 15-year-old boys (10.71 seconds). Yet, some people want equality in broadcasting and compensation between men's and women's professional sports. While it is essential to give women the same access to sports as men, why should competition magically attract as many women as men?

To flatten wages and establish parity, wokeism must necessarily deny differences in skill and performance. In the woke sports spectacle, celebrating diversity supplants admiring excellence.

Woke and feminist ideologies share a common mission to deconstruct everything that defines an individual's identity. They represent powerful syncretisms of absurd thinking and egalitarianism. If successful, they would render society's members undifferentiated, creolized, and androgynous – ultimately resembling an anthill or beehive, the quintessential forms of matriarchal organization.

The uniqueness of individuals, the wellspring of innovation and adaptation (reduction of entropy through the creation of new knowledge), would be sacrificed for the efficiency of a perfectly coherent and static society. Living species favor cooperation over competition when adapting to scarcity.

Traditional societies, subject to chronic scarcity due to the lack of industrial processes, rely more on cooperation. In South Africa, the word "ubuntu," adopted by the free software community Linux, expresses this interconnection between individual existence and group belonging. It becomes evident that collectivist regimes maintain scarcity through the ideology of cooperation and suppress the spirit of competition that might otherwise generate abundance.

"There is neither Jew nor Greek, there is neither slave nor free, there is neither male nor female; for you are all one in Jesus Christ."

– Saint Paul, Galatians 3:28

This Christian quote contrasts with Confucian thought, which sees all humans as part of the same family but arranged in hierarchical relationships based on age, education, and wisdom, criteria that are inherently unequal. Anyone attempting to level human relations in terms of education and wisdom inevitably resorts to relativism, preserves the worst traditions, and engages in a totalitarian approach consistent with an unquestionable religious discourse.

26. Empire

Empire: "A vast assembly of countries dependent on the same authority, whether or not it is exercised by an emperor."

The word *empire*, phonetically associated with the verb "empirer" in French (to worsen), carries a premonition of inevitable decline. Every empire reaches its peak before collapsing.

According to historian and philosopher Yuval Harari, the empire represents the ultimate and optimal political organization for maximizing the wealth and well-being of its members – a world government where localism would find its balance with the effects of globalization.

Empires are protean, sometimes founded on individualism like the American Empire, sometimes on collectivism like China, but always sustained by a feeling of superiority over other states–an imperial nationalism.

To illustrate the power of decentralization, let's compare the fate of two particularly deadly ideologies: Nazism and communism. Nazism, centralized around a *Führer*, was effectively eradicated, while communism, globalized through proliferation, escaped any trial despite disastrous outcomes. The Nuremberg Trials corresponded to the ideological eradication of Nazism, but communism's Nuremberg has yet to materialize. Similarly, Islam, thanks to the decentralization of its clergy, conveniently escapes criticism of Islamism, which, like the Hydra of mythology, is reborn after its misdeeds and defeats.

The empire exemplifies the political dissipative structure that perfectly illustrates the third principle: the maximization of energy flow by reducing internal entropy, peak followed by implosion.

The Roman Empire's population around 150 CE is estimated at 75 million – fewer inhabitants than modern Germany. Yet, today's globalists harbor the grandiose ambition to control a world population approaching 8 billion humans through a world government with the World Economic Forum (WEF) as its foundational body.

To achieve this, under the banner of efficiency, they work to abolish borders and promote migrations, creating interchangeable, more malleable subjects stripped of their ancestral cultures. They cloak themselves in virtue redefined by wokeism.

Adam Smith warned that "virtue should be feared more than vice because its excesses are not subject to the regulation of conscience." Giscard became the first French president to publicly advocate for a globalized society as early as 1974.

This excerpt from Luc-Olivier d'Algange's essay, *Refractory Thoughts*, reveals the unavowed objective of these policies: to establish a standardized world order, erase local cultures to make the world a vast shopping mall whose slogan will be "come as you are"; niche marketing will handle particularities, and mass marketing will serve mass production. He urged:

> *The interchangeable is not only the condition for the functioning of the globalized world but, if one dares say, profaning such a noble word, its vocation. This world operates by the interchangeable and for the interchangeable, that is to say, against the tragic feeling that accompanies the living joy of the irreplaceable nature of beings and things....Through the generalization of the interchangeable, the Moderns cultivate the illusion of conquering death by plunging us into a world resembling it. Thus it wants to triumph the fallacious security of boredom, by simultaneously discarding both the tragic and the joy.*

Local governments will gradually surrender their powers to the world government. Winter gatherings at Davos foster the illusion not only that this world government could exist, but that its participants merit inclusion.

A corollary of this dystopia is natalism and the inability to accept the consequence of increased life expectancy, namely, the aging of the population. Globalists prefer the young, who consume more, especially when they have young children. With controlled birth rates, there wouldn't really be fewer young people, but they would represent a smaller percentage of the general population.

Still, this prospect frightens the globalists. Thus, the French social security system operates on a pay-as-you-go basis. Schematically, the working population pays for the retirees. This arrangement becomes precarious if productivity gains fail to offset active worker scarcity. For about ten years, France's birth rate has declined from 830,000 to 725,000 births annually between 2010 and 2022, according to INSEE. And in 2023, the drop is even sharper, with a decrease of 7% compared to 2022. Recall that below 2.07 children per woman, the population begins to decline in the long term. Moreover, people over 60 receive more social benefits (pensions, healthcare, and dependency) than young workers, which amplifies the effect of the relative aging of the population.

Artificial intelligence and frugality could provide an escape from this dilemma. AI is both the electrification of processes and the robotization of tasks while using collected data to learn and improve. Frugality consists of moderating our appetite for new things to preserve access to essential ones. The crucial questions become: How will AI-related productivity gains be applied? Will they foster a more frugal, less youth-centric world, or will they perpetuate population growth and consumption?

In December 2023, during France's immigration law debate and vote, Medef president Patrick Martin expressly favored the latter option:

> *In the Nordic countries where the debate has been objectively posed, it is not the employers who massively demand immigration; it's the economy. ... By 2050, we would need, unless we reinvent our social model, unless we reinvent our economic model, 3,900,000 foreign workers. ... All countries of the European Union are facing this demographic problem.*

Note how this globalist logic conveniently attributed the purported "need for millions of foreign workers" to an abstract, non-existent entity. The logic thus becomes indisputable because one does not argue with the economy.

If we were to talk about the needs of the people or, worse for the Medef, their desires, we would have to consult them, which globalists prefer to avoid. Moreover, even during a referendum, voting results are thoroughly flouted in a sort of double blow: the globalists achieve their ends while claiming that the people were consulted. A democracy where the people are consulted but not listened to is a regime of consultants where McKinsey law rules.

With the dilution of the value of work following unbridled monetary creation, the salaries of professions (agriculture, health, education, security) are no longer attractive enough, while, comparatively, the salaries of managers (bankers, consultants, senior civil servants) are pushed upward by the Cantillon effect. That's why the Medef and its "economy," and not the people, need cheap imported labor.

They have no use for the local culture but instead wish to replace it with an absence of culture – a globalized mishmash that will serve as a cultural substrate for docile consumers of standardized products. The aisles of a shopping center in Doha are indistinguishable from those in New York, Paris, or Tokyo.

From a thermodynamic point of view, the creolization of society, the erasure of regional or local culture, and its replacement by a globalist subculture can be seen as a reduction of entropy at the species level. If there is only one culture, there is no longer friction between cultures.

We arrive at the fallacious security of boredom, as Luc-Olivier d'Algange previously wrote. Mitterrand, Giscard's successor, claimed that "nationalism is war," but one could just as well say that nationalism is peace. Swiss neutrality relies on its nationalism. Indeed, alliances between friendly states caused the outbreak of the First World War. The famous parochialism brandished by globalists to caricature patriotism could have then saved peace and triggered a local war rather than a world one.

Today, admitting Ukraine to NATO could trigger a new world war. In the same vein, globalists credit European institutions with maintaining peace since their inception, except for the war in Serbia. So, one could equally assert that the European Union was born thanks to the peace of nations.

Western, Middle Eastern, and Eastern cultures, however, do not converge. When cultures coexist without converging – that is, when there is no assimilation with the local culture – natural selection applies with all its harshness. And if we must keep the best and reject the worst of each of them, no one has the legitimacy, much less the authority, to make the selection. The world government does not exist, and meanwhile, the WEF and its stable of "young global leaders" handle current affairs and pursue their interchangeable utopia–an empire built not on shared values but on the systematic erasure of difference itself.

27. Humanity

Humanity: "A disposition toward understanding and compassion for one's fellow beings, which leads to helping those in need: Treat someone with humanity."

Let us approach with skepticism any grand proclamations claiming to return the "human" to the center of social systems. Such rhetoric often conceals an agenda behind the guise of the common good, aiming to subjugate individuals under the arbitrary rule of an oligarchy or a supposedly benevolent despot.

Emotions and cognitive biases are algorithms of fast thinking, as described by Kahneman and Harari, that produce predictable results. Fear triggers flight or defense behaviors. Love, oscillating between control over the other and self-renunciation, produces behaviors that connect us to others. Only reasoning frees us from the determinism of emotions by offering alternative options.

This capacity for reason distinguishes us as a species, while our emotions are easily observed in the animal world, where they appear more touching in their primordial innocence. Nothing equals the unconditional love of a dog for its master.

Love between two beings boils down to a bidirectional flow of energy. It can thus create dependence or result from it, which leads some to relativize love in the animal world. Imagining love between humans as superior and transcendent is an anthropocentric bias.

We must also understand what distinguishes us from objects. As early as 1941, Isaac Asimov published a short story ("Liar!", later integrated into the *I, Robot* series) in which he proposed three rules applicable to any robot, implicitly defining a boundary between the machine and its creator. First, a robot must not harm a human being, even through inaction. Second, it must obey orders given by a qualified human unless the orders violate the first rule. Third, it must protect its own existence as long as this does not violate the first or second rule.

After all, the emergence of artificial intelligence reminds us that the boundaries between dissipative structures are very blurred, even if our natural anthropomorphism would like them to be impassable.

Buddhism identifies five *skandhas* constituting a human being: body, sensation, perception, mental formation, and consciousness. In this symbolism, the body is a stock of energy capable of capturing an energy flow. Sensations are a capture of information, and perceptions are a reduction of entropy thanks to the information captured. Mental formations refer to the manifestations of will responding to perceptions and sensations. They implement the third principle at the individual or collective level.

Karma is inscribed in the mental formations. It is the course of actions determined by the body, perceptions, and sensations. Consciousness is the perception of the context of observation, synthesizing perceptions and manifestations of will.

The impermanence of beings and things is central in Buddhist philosophy, which considers the assembly of these skandhas, which constitute being and self, as temporary.

According to François Roddier, living beings exist in a thermodynamic, stationary state out of equilibrium. An increase in entropy corresponds to a loss of information about what is going to happen. By definition, information reduces unpredictability.

A train that arrives on time does not constitute information, neither in the thermodynamic sense nor in the journalistic sense. However, knowledge of an animal on the railway tracks provides information that reduces the observer's entropy because it allows them to predict that the train will be late. Conversely, if the presence of the animal is not detected, ignorance generates an increase in entropy for the observer.

A sense of responsibility is the sole characteristic that distinguishes a human from an algorithm. An algorithm does not naturally feel solidarity with another algorithm, much less with a human. Humans have this innate or acquired sense, but not all of them, far from it, which makes the distinction between human and artificial intelligence uncertain. Moreover, a computer protocol, especially for a peer-to-peer network like Bitcoin, can establish a form of cooperation between machines. One could say that humans have a natural capacity to form societies, which machines have yet to grasp, but let's wager that it's within their reach.

Intelligence is no longer a criterion for distinguishing humans as AI progresses. The learning capacities and, thus, adaptation of machines have surpassed those of humans.

Agility, the ability to pivot from one specialization to another, remains a uniquely human asset, one difficult to transpose to machines that cannot reprogram themselves without altering their use and nature.

In *Adages*, Erasmus speaks to us about free will, another supposedly distinctive characteristic of humans. Erasmus criticizes Luther's Protestantism on the grounds that the denial of free will compromises ethics. There would be no ethics without responsibility and no responsibility without free will.

The human condition truly differs from the so-called "animal" condition only by the complexity and extent of our capacities, which compels us to seek excellence. Complexity is itself a consequence of the third principle, which states that dissipative structures, starting from elementary particles, self-organize by forming new, ever more complex structures.

What we call culture is the spectacular emanation of this complexity. Culture reduces the entropy of the species by transmitting knowledge from one generation to the next. Cultural evolution multiplies the effect of cognitive abilities enhanced by biological evolution.

According to the composer Edgar Varèse (1883–1965), cited by John Welford: "An artist is never ahead of his time, but most people are behind theirs."

For the anthropologist David Graeber, "abandoning the narrative of primordial innocence does not mean giving up on dreams of human emancipation – that is, of a society where no one can use their wealth to enslave others or to say that their lives and needs do not matter."

Wars, often described as inhuman, even though they are recurring markers of history, appear as a phenomenon of expansion and contraction of human societies, a typical energy behavior. "Yang" energy is expressed through the spirit of conquest but sacrifices itself for the "Yin," the spirit of cooperation that emerges from the necessity of reconstruction after destruction.

To illustrate the increasing energy capture of the species, the English merchant navy in 1582 had a 68,000-ton capacity requiring 16,000 sailors. By contrast, in 2017, the container ship *OOCL Hong Kong*, the largest built to date, boasted a capacity of 200,000 tons yet operated with a crew of only 22 sailors.

The notion of waste is intimately linked to that of monopoly. Without a monopoly, everyone uses the currency of their choice, and any unused currency is perceived as a waste.

Every issuance of currency is the monetization of a form of energy and social credit. Social credit represents community acceptance of that currency, which is necessary for any data to become information. Though currency today has evolved into digital data, it remains subject to this requirement. Promise-money needs a maximum number of believers, whereas proof-money relies only on verifiers. Let's not forget, indeed, that entropy is measured for an observer (an individual or a group). Without users, there is no observer, and without an observer, no entropy reduction.

For promise-money, the reduction of entropy occurs through banks. They draw an energetic benefit by charging interest on monetary creation via credit, as they do not supply the energy counterpart. This comes from the borrower. Indeed, it is the work of the borrower that underpins the promise of payment of future installments.

With proof-money, each user can verify their own transactions and thus reduce their entropy, with the resulting thermodynamic benefit. Creating proof-money fundamentally differs from promise-money by its energy counterpart and profit margins. Unlike banks that source energy from the borrower, Bitcoin miners themselves provide the energy counterpart of monetary creation, as they must use electricity to validate each new block through computation. The miner who validates a block receives a reward in bitcoins but must resell a large part of it to pay their electricity bills. In doing so, they inject this monetary creation into the economy via the energy sector.

Banks inject monetary creation by granting credit to borrowers, but it is indeed the borrowers who provide the energy counterpart by working to repay their debts. Unlike commercial banks, which are in an oligopoly position in monetary creation through credit, Bitcoin validators operate with low margins since they are in global competition. The protocol incentivizes continuous geographical arbitrage to locate the cheapest electricity, typically unused production surpluses.

Evolution has produced complementary human dispositions: believers versus skeptics and introverts versus extroverts. The differences appear more innate than acquired.

Recent research highlights the role of two substances produced by the brain (neurotransmitters), dopamine and acetylcholine, that determine different personality types.

Dopamine excites and satisfies extroverts during risk-taking or social encounters, while introverts feel overstimulated, making them uncomfortable and anxious. To release acetylcholine in their brains, introverts read, concentrate, and focus their minds on problem-solving, which relaxes, satisfies, and motivates them. They maintain fewer friendships but forge deeper connections.

What distinguishes an introvert from an extrovert? The introvert strives to reduce collective entropy through the acquisition of knowledge to self-organize the species, while the extrovert seeks to establish as many connections as possible with their environment to reduce their entropy at the individual level. This duality of dissipative structures – simultaneously an individual and a member of a species – characterizes living beings.

Similarly, when the young replace the old at the species level, their energy replaces more or less static information, namely, the experience and culture of the elders who have already produced an entropy-reducing effect.

The self-righteous are never lacking when it comes to speaking of the good and, if possible, taking on a noble role in the process. For example, according to the Forum for Other Indicators of Wealth (FAIR),

"Cooperation and solidarity are to human societies what biodiversity is to life: what allows us to overcome shocks." In reality, cooperation is necessary when there is scarcity, but in times of abundance, the law of Maximum Entropy Production (MEP) indicates that competition prevails. Passing moral judgment on these behaviors ("competition is bad, cooperation is good") rigidifies society and reduces its resilience – that natural agility that allows adaptation.

To be convinced of this, one must understand that life, like any dissipative structure, operates through phases of expansion and contraction. In other words, nature is subject to energy fluctuations. Sleep is an example of this succession of phases. After capturing energy and information during the day, sleep reduces the organism's entropy, lowering its temperature and transforming information into knowledge.

The behavior of a sandpile onto which a flow of sand is poured illustrates this as well. The height of the pile will fluctuate around a critical value. The pile is never in equilibrium at this precise height, but as soon as it is exceeded, an avalanche of sand grains can occur at any moment. The avalanche brings the height of the pile below the critical height and starts to increase again until the next fluctuation. We should think of sleep as this avalanche. The flow of energy is continuous, but the dissipative structure (living being or sandpile) operates intermittently in fits and starts. For humans, this manifests as wakefulness and sleep; for the sandpile, growth and avalanche.

Every living being is part of a species that is itself an open system and, therefore, subject to fluctuations, which also explains the reproduction of individuals and their death. If deaths outnumber births, we sometimes observe the extinction of a species or even a mass extinction that affects more or less all species, the living world itself being an open system. A static equilibrium for an open system corresponds to death. Life, on the other hand, is characterized by oscillations of measurable variables around critical values out of any equilibrium.

In summary, open systems are subject to fluctuation, and open systems are nested within each other, from the infinitely small (elementary particles) to the infinitely large (the observable universe). Humans, living beings, and nature in the broad sense – including mountains and oceans – are aspects of the same emerging reality.

How can we not despair at ultimately being only energy converters deprived of eternal life? The extraordinary does not become ordinary on the pretext that it can be explained. We belong to the species that has taken control of an incredible planet. What distinguishes us, failing to save us from a certain end, is the capacity for wonder and the gratitude for having received such a generous lot, even if nothing and no one is responsible for this fate.

Paul Desalmand remarked in *Atheism Explained* that "if theologians have so firmly held to the idea of man as the purpose of the universe, it's because they well understood what would result from the opposite. If man is not the purpose of the universe, it's probably because this universe has none."

28. Identity

Identity: "The permanent and fundamental character of someone, or a group, which defines their individuality, their uniqueness: A person searching for their identity. National identity. The set of factual and legal data that allows someone to be individualized (date and place of birth, name, first name, parentage, etc.)."

Heraclitus believed that one could not bathe twice in the same river because it is always changing. If he bought a cow, someone might challenge his ownership by claiming that the animal had changed and was no longer the same as the one he purchased. This impermanence of things and beings, central to Buddhist philosophy, leads to the definition of identity as the invariant foundation of a changing being.

From another perspective, the science of energy teaches us that the more complex an open system is, the more unpredictable its behavior becomes. The difficulty in predicting the weather a week in advance reflects the complexity of the meteorological system, composed of the atmosphere, the ocean, solar radiation, etc.

A human being is also a complex system and, therefore, largely unpredictable. The definition of identity results from a process that cannot rely on a fixed image of the person.

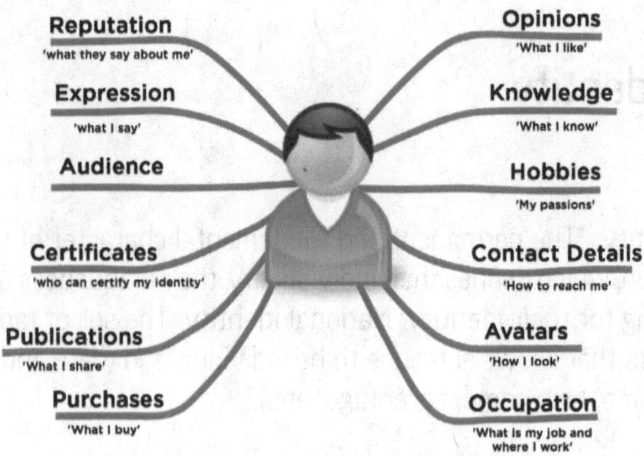

What Defines Our Identity?

The knowledge of the other allows us to reduce our uncertainty about their behavior. The set of data that contributes to this knowledge constitutes the identity of the other.

Identity is, by nature, self-sovereign. Every human being is the source of their own identity and should remain at the center of their management.

For John Locke, identity is primarily based on memory, but consciousness goes beyond this restrictive conception.

Consciousness, which defines our identity, is the ability to position oneself between the past and the future and between different unfoldings of the present. It can also be defined as the capacity to observe one's own thoughts as phenomena. It becomes clear that it is difficult to define identity as simply the reflection of individual consciousness, as it would then be almost independent of context.

However, in line with our analysis of living beings as essentially subject to the principles of thermodynamics, identity appears as a synthesis of the entropic state of the individual.

Let us recall that entropy is a state function that characterizes an observer's uncertainty regarding the evolution of their environment. Identity describes this state in that context. Its understanding reduces the unpredictability of the evolution and behavior of a complex being. However, as human beings become more predictable, they also become an easier target for merchants looking to sell their products.

Some companies understand this dynamic very well. By encouraging frenzied self-exposure and identity performances on social networks, their goal is nothing less than the increasingly sophisticated collection of increasingly detailed data, like an endless series of forms that are continuously being filled out.

For example, an individual's identity will take a very different form depending on whether they live in a developed country or in the heart of an equatorial forest. In a developed country, identity consists of proof of belonging to various communities: human, with information such as date of birth, name, and surname; professional, with a declaration of occupation; national, with a passport; and local, with proof of residence. In an equatorial forest, identity might be summarized by belonging to a tribe and a profession expressed through ornaments or attributes.

If identity is modeled as a set of data, every piece of data derives its value and meaning from its context. This is why there can be no precise definition of identity, only a cataloging of the information that can constitute a certain identity in a given context.

If an individual's identity allows us to know them better, can the notion of identity apply to a group to define a people or a nation? The answer to this question reflects a political worldview with two extreme positions.

On one side are cultural relativists, who believe that all cultures are equal and aim for a generalized global melting pot where they blend to form an indistinguishable blob. They reject any hierarchy of cultures because they deny the existence of objective criteria to rank them. There is also no room for cultural identity, as the very notion of identity is too relativized and distorted to be defined. This ideology strips humans of everything that constitutes them, starting with their identity.

On the other side are the identitarians, who believe that a local culture, inherited from a past when humans moved more slowly than today, significantly defines an individual's identity. For them, the traces of artistic heritage left by a culture distinguish it from others, and in this regard, not all cultures are equal. The individual is thus justified in defending their identity as a group identity, primarily cultural, tied to their territorial homeland.

When existing borders around a national territory are abolished, one can expect new borders to emerge within that territory – a phenomenon referred to as communitarianism. A culture integrates individuals, not communities. If a community arrives with its own culture without assimilating, its culture is juxtaposed rather than added to the local culture. The immigrant then becomes an occupant. Cohesion gives way to the fragmentation of society.

A self-sovereign identity is essential for the protection of privacy. Only the individual can protect their own data by choosing to disclose it based solely on the need to know. No justification can sustainably challenge the freedom of an individual to control their own data.

Renowned cryptographer and educator Bruce Schneier emphasized the importance of individual digital sovereignty:

> *Despite alarmist rhetoric to the contrary, terrorism is not a transcendent threat. A terrorist attack cannot destroy a country's way of life; only our response to such an attack can cause that kind of damage. The more we distort our own laws, the more we turn our buildings into fortresses, the more we reduce our freedoms and the freedoms that founded our societies, the more we do the terrorists' work for them.*

Wokeism in the private sphere is the counterpart to globalism in the economic domain. Both reflect an ethereal vision of the human condition. Just as globalism falsely assumes that the lifestyle of the digital nomad can be universally applied without obstacles or harm, wokeism dazzles gullible people with the illusion of effortlessly traveling between different identities to the point where they no longer know which one truly defines them. Identity touches our innate essence, but it does not determine our unique existence, which is shaped by our experiences and our freedom.

The Darwinian differentiation of the sexes has led to the predominance of Yin in women and Yang in men. An unfortunate consequence of this statistical reality is that Yin is sometimes confused with feminine essence and Yang with the emanation of a masculine character.

In reality, Yin and Yang coexist within every individual, in varying proportions from one person to another and from one period of life to the next. Combating prejudices and ideologies such as feminism involves aspiring to a higher level of consciousness, which allows one to recognize in oneself and in others when and how Yin or Yang manifests, depending on life's circumstances. This duality of Yin and Yang, as theorized by Taoism, seems far more philosophically fruitful to me than the mythological representation of Mars and Venus, which is too reductive and sexually connoted. Yin encompasses the feminine but is not confined to the dimension of gender.

David Salle, a postmodernist painter, advises: "Be an anthropologist of your own universe."

Many classical philosophers have sought to model the duality of energy through concepts that are more or less obscure. For Spinoza, for example, everything identifies itself by its formal essence–its materiality perceived through the senses–and by its objective essence, understood by reason. Like many renowned philosophers, he refers to energy without naming it as a unique substance, which the prism of the mind separates into a flow of reasonings, or thought, on the one hand, and a flow of perceptions, or physical extension, on the other.

Identity and Rights

For General de Gaulle, it was "France first, then the State, and finally the law."

Under the pressure of the third law of thermodynamics, the efficiency of globalism has overtaken the resilience of the regional and local. This is why ideologies aimed at deconstructing any identity tied to locality and origins have found sponsors supporting this movement. An efficient world, but one severed from its roots, is populated by individuals who have gradually been stripped of their individual rights (identity, property), in exchange for being granted social rights.

Once globalized, social rights provide the foundation for a world governance that elites have long dreamed of exercising. Such power, detached from the needs of a people that must be satisfied to secure votes, can be attained and maintained through co-optation and insularity.

The obsession with avoiding discrimination eventually leads to the disappearance of concepts like discernment, desire, and preference. Bureaucratic managers seek to impose on employers and innovators even the choice of their collaborators, as if businesses were reduced to mere administrations.

Law becomes an unchecked power when, independent of the executive branch, it ends up controlling it through regulatory capture. At that point, law opposes true justice. In France, for example, property rights have significantly regressed in favor of squatters. The weakening of property rights is a strong indicator of a country's descent into third-world conditions. Property rights represent a reduction in entropy for the individual, a guarantee of well-being, and a lever for capturing more energy.

It took mobilizing the media through a few courageous journalists who denounced the harms caused by squatters for the legislators to take notice and provide better protections for small property owners.

Identity and Globalization

As François Roddier emphasized, living species adapt their behaviors by alternating between cooperation during times of scarcity and competition during periods of abundance, in a contraction-expansion cycle, a typical feature of dissipative structures.

Globalization, orchestrated by countries where abundance reigns, has crushed cooperation where it was most needed due to scarcity. This harmful distortion has only been made possible by wrapping it in moral considerations.

According to Pierre-Marie Lledo:

> *On an evolutionary level, morality appears as an extreme form of cooperation that demands individuals to suppress*

> *their own interests or assimilate them to those of others. Studies of primate and child behavior show the conserved nature of this trait. They indicate that cooperation first arises from a personal morality centered on the individual and their close relations. Then, as a kind of extension of this personal morality, a universal morality emerges. It is from this second stage that individuals follow and apply the social norms of the group. Morality thus emerged over the course of species evolution, becoming more complex, starting with a set of skills and motivations to cooperate first with kin, and then with everyone.*

When morality meets ideology, it results in virtue signaling, with its hallmarks, including cultural relativism as a misunderstood version of tolerance, lack of discernment as an inability to pick up on weak signals and filter strong ones, denial of reality, and finally, an obsession with reputation.

Identity and Immigration

Can we imagine a debate on road safety focused on the pros and cons of automobiles while only marginally addressing speed limits? Yet, this is exactly what happens in discussions about immigration. Any conversation about controlling migration flows instantly turns into a debate on the humanity and morality of immigration.

It's evident that when migrants arrive too quickly and in too great numbers, fleeing countries plagued by lawlessness, corruption, and violence, they cannot assimilate properly. Before assimilation comes integration, and before integration, there must be acceptance.

Migrants from Buddhist or Confucian cultures face no issues of acceptance, but not all cultures are compatible with each other. A culture asserts an identity, and such assertions can be contradictory. With massive non-European immigration, European peoples are being subjected to the same strategy of cultural dilution that China applies to Tibet with the Han Chinese.

Central banks need growth to continue fueling their monopolistic systems. Demographic growth, providing cheap human labor, has supplanted economic growth previously reliant on the exploitation of cheap fossil fuels.

Public authorities are subjected to both the implicit demands of central banks and temporal preferences. The cost of controlling immigration must be paid now, whereas the costs of uncontrolled immigration accumulate over several generations. The pressure from banks on political decisions can be explicit. When the Tunisian president questioned Sub-Saharan immigration in his country in March 2023, the World Bank immediately responded by threatening to cut aid to Tunisia.

In his novel *Anéantir*, Michel Houellebecq observes:

> *Artificial reproduction and immigration were the two means used by contemporary societies to compensate for the decline in their fertility rates. Modern countries like Japan and Korea leaned toward artificial reproduction, while less technologically advanced countries, like those in Western Europe, resorted to immigration. In both cases, the goal sought by capitalism was achieved: a slow but steady increase in the global population, which allowed growth targets to be met and ensured a decent return on investments. Only an eco-fascist ideology like that of Savitri Devi, or an openly degrowth and primitivist one like Kaczynski's, with a synthesis of the two being conceivable, represented an alternative. These movements could furthermore be considered close to nihilism, insofar as they aimed primarily at the establishment of chaos, convinced that the world resulting from it would necessarily be better.*

Politicians unwilling to solve specific problems link them to larger, less tractable issues – inverting methodical approaches. To solve a difficult problem, Descartes advised breaking it down into several smaller, more manageable problems. Einstein counseled, "Avoid negative people; they always have a problem for every solution."

The pragmatist tries to find solutions to real-world problems. The ideologue imposes a doctrine onto reality and then attempts to distort it – often through lies, sometimes through dictatorship – to make it fit their ideology. Reality changes, but the ideology does not, which means it has no limits.

For example, the journalist Charlotte d'Ornellas describes the consequences of an ideological approach to immigration:

> *Many figures, generally aligned with the right, comment on, describe, and warn about the inevitable consequences of massive, uncontrolled immigration, encouraged and paired with a multicultural and victimhood narrative. No one wanted to believe them; many preferred to demonize the messenger rather than face the harshness of the message.*

This highlights the danger of adhering too rigidly to ideology when confronting complex and evolving societal issues like immigration.

Identity and Reputation

For an observer, my reputation measures the energy I have used for useful purposes from their perspective. As information, reputation, like value or entropy, is relative.

The value of information thus depends on the reputation of its source. A source deemed reliable is, by definition, an entropy reducer for its audience. According to the second law of thermodynamics, verifying information consumes energy.

Nicky Case's *trust game* experiment demonstrated that three elements are needed to foster cooperation strategies and social trust: repeated interactions, the possibility of mutual gain (a non-zero-sum game, meaning win-win), and few communication errors. He concluded, "Our problem today is that our environment works against the evolution of trust. We are the environment for others. In the short term, the game defines the players. But in the long term, we, the players, define the game."

In other words, instead of lamenting the harms of capitalism, we should focus on building relationships, offering win-win exchanges, and communicating clearly. Building lasting and close connections rather than opportunistic and distant relationships means favoring local identity and historical continuity rather than the insane logic of globalization and immigrationism.

From the complexity of beings comes the diversity of strategies, but trust and cooperation arise from the stability of the parties involved.

Ultimately, a point-based reputation system (social credit) may be preferable to a purely qualitative, informal, arbitrary, and opaque reputation system. The real issue lies in the potential for its misuse by authorities, whether elected or unelected, with extensive powers.

Identity, Uniqueness, Unpredictability

A dynamic system is said to be chaotic when its evolution depends heavily on initial conditions. The experiment of the turbulent fountain illustrates chaos theory: each drop of water plays its role, but it's impossible to predict the direction of rotation in the long term, even with the world's most powerful computer.

The butterfly effect, described by Edward Lorenz, is another example. A chaotic system is not necessarily highly complex, but the reverse is not true. The evolution of a complex system is inherently unpredictable, and from complexity arises the uniqueness of behaviors and characteristics.

The identity of an animal is relatively straightforward because the animal remains predictable compared to a human, whose identity is, by nature, more complex to define.

Identity, Anonymity, and Fame

Anonymity or pseudonymity are modalities of a self-sovereign identity. They allow for debate without one's ideas being categorized or judged before they are heard or understood.

The media exposure of a celebrity, while it may lead to a broader knowledge of their person, ultimately results in their desanctification. Every idea they express is then blurred by the identity of its source, as if obscured by a smoke screen.

29. Freedom

Liberty: "The state of someone who is not subject to a master. The condition of a people that governs itself with full sovereignty. The situation of someone who determines themselves without any external pressure or prejudice. The state of someone who is not bound by a contractual, marital, or sentimental commitment."

Synonyms: autonomy, independence, latitude.

Benjamin Constant describes it as the fragile balance between the assertion of a majority and the protection of a minority: "By liberty, I mean the triumph of individuality both over the authority that seeks to govern through despotism and over the masses that demand the right to enslave the minority."

France, reputed to be liberty's homeland, is one of the rare countries, perhaps the only one, to have committed both regicide and populicide. The King was guillotined in 1793. Its people are now slowly being killed by globalization that took hold in the 1970s.

Liberty is the luxury of the human species. At the top of the food chain, the apex predator can aspire to autonomy, at least within the limits of its peers' autonomy. Freedom exists only within the species. When isolated, the individual is constrained by elements and natural forces beyond their control. In a group, they depend on others through specialization and the division of labor.

Progress is merely the expression of the third law of thermodynamics, aiming to maximize energy flow, both individually and collectively, through self-organization and reducing entropy. When society is caught in a suddenly increased flow, such as during a war aiming to reduce its entropy (uncertainty about its environment's evolution, for example, the behavior of a neighboring or colonized country), the individual flow is put in the service of the army.

Progress is not inherently emancipatory. It frees us from certain constraints only to create others, as Henry David Thoreau emphasized in his writings advocating for voluntary simplicity, closer to nature and away from society. Its effects are more evident in the energy flow at the species level (extended life expectancy, increasing the amount of energy transformed through economic activity) than in the liberation of the individual.

Freedom and Circulation

Hunting (or rather hunting accidents) raises the question of space free from constraints – in this case, safety constraints. The space occupied by a hunter, where the safety of a passerby is reduced by the presence of the hunter, is a sphere with a radius equal to the range of the hunter's rifle. The same applies to motorcyclists. The surface area they occupy when the motorcycle is stationary is much smaller compared to a car but much larger when speeding through a city. Thus, the space occupied by the motorcycle becomes an arc with a radius equal to its braking distance (including the rider's reaction time).

Liberty often stands in opposition to authority. Libertarians, when identified as such, do not hesitate to speak of "authoritarians in denial." Authority should not be a power with objectives, but rather a resource people consult to solve a problem.

Freedom of Expression, Freedom to Undertake

Education is defined by the ability to understand an idea without necessarily adopting it. This is a prerequisite for any freedom of expression.

As the infamous Ugandan dictator Idi Amin Dada warned, "Freedom of speech exists, but I cannot guarantee freedom after speech." In contrast, a comedian observed that freedom of speech only wears out if you don't use it. Even those with nothing to say must defend freedom of speech, just as privacy must be protected even by those with nothing to hide.

Surveillance tools can sooner or later fall into the wrong hands. The election process, often equated with democracy, can bring to power a totalitarian government that sacrifices freedom in the name of security.

The right to property and education are the foundations of the freedom to undertake. The right to property and the protection of privacy stem from the same individual liberty – the right to privatize a stock or flow of energy. Material goods are energy stocks, while privacy represents the portion of energy or information flow that an individual captures outside the public sphere.

The flow of information is indeed equivalent to a flow of energy captured or saved. According to the conservation principle, information that is replicated does not allow the replication of an amount of energy. It only affects how energy circulates. For example, when our hiker saves energy thanks to GPS information, they can use the saved energy – primarily chemical energy from food – for something other than finding their way. They do not receive additional energy. However, if they use information to find food, it enables them to capture additional energy. Information thus operates through two levers: one on capturing additional energy and the other on energy savings.

The right to property temporarily stabilizes our environment, reduces stress, and brings us closer to thermodynamic equilibrium. This is achieved by eliminating an energy flow for the owner, namely, the monetary outflow of rent. In modern societies, the individual is caught between the psychopathic corporation and the neurotic administration. The psychopathic corporation justifies the disappearance of competitors in the name of competition, while the administration seeks to eliminate not competition but to suppress freedom–anything that escapes its control.

Democracy's downward spiral begins when it grants the privilege of public speech, a privilege that must be preserved by conforming to accepted norms. Political correctness becomes the benchmark for consensual public discourse – the kind that, appearing virtuous, enables one to be elected.

The system inevitably permits only speech that aligns with its own preservation. As legal protections expand, they do so at the expense of liberty. Laws begin to drift when individual freedom is so constrained by the freedom of others that everyone loses out. The system, in turn, can only produce laws aligned with the objective of its own preservation.

Increasingly, the downward spiral of law can be seen in daily life:

- Terms and conditions of use or sale that are so lengthy that it would take several days to read and are therefore accepted under duress;
- The gradual deconstruction of national borders;
- Arbitrary delisting by digital platforms, without any possibility of recourse;
- Sudden closure of accounts (bank or otherwise) without reason or notice;
- Small businesses and producers have their brands and trademarks plundered by larger players armed with legal firepower. Google, for example, auctions off registered trademarks to advertisers, who are often competitors of those brands.

Through rigid legalism, centralized software-driven economies establish absolute administrative power by making it anonymous and beyond the reach of the individual.

Decentralization and education are the two prerequisites for digital sovereignty. Decentralization removes reliance on central authorities, while education is essential because decentralized systems often appear less convenient than their centralized counterparts. To foster adoption, users must understand the benefits of digital sovereignty and best practices, particularly regarding the security of private keys.

Freedom and Equality

Rather than striving for equality of opportunity, which is difficult to define, shouldn't the role of public power be to ensure a diversity of opportunities and a fair recognition of talent?

By constantly denying merit to prevent it from turning into domination, the group's entropy is increased to the point of stagnation and despair. When mastery and talent no longer provide a path for advancement, all that remains is the collusion and arbitrariness of the egalitarians.

Freedom and the Right to Property

Should freedom of movement be based on the certainty of hospitality, as immigration advocates implicitly suggest?

By offering their land to a multitude of new arrivals, Westerners accept a retreat in the right to collective property, the ownership of the common areas of their country. But, private property rights are also being eroded even faster through legal mechanisms, specifically through legal discrepancies. The strengthening of tenants' rights in relation to their landlords illustrates this shift.

The decline in private property rights corresponds to the transformation of an energy stock, ownership of an asset, into an energy flow, the rental of that asset. The landlord is no longer an individual saver but a collective, usually a state or a large multinational corporation. This decline mirrors an overall trend—the shift from ownership (an energy stock) to rental (an energy flow). For instance, we increasingly own fewer physical books, records, or movies and instead rent from Amazon Kindle, Netflix, or Spotify. Younger generations are finding it harder to acquire homes and are often stuck in the position of renters. In France, the state now offers electric car leases for 100 euros a month, following a trend where nearly one in two private cars were already being leased in 2023. Despite this, the majority of drivers would still prefer to purchase their vehicles.

Substituting rental for ownership is, in fact, an openly stated goal of the World Economic Forum (WEF): "You will own nothing, and you will be happy," predicted Danish politician Ida Auken in 2016.

Do we still have the freedom to project ourselves into a chosen future, or are we forced to endure a civilizational shift due to migratory waves?

In Indian society, the Brahmins are at the top of the caste hierarchy. They are supposed to attain a higher form of freedom by renouncing material wealth. Similarly, the right to private property provides a form of individual control over the future, but at the cost of security guaranteed by the group.

In democratic societies, we rely on elected officials to create laws, but the process of universal suffrage is inherently tied to ideology. By offering a guiding framework, ideological, ready-made thinking allows a political program to be presented to the masses in a digestible way. Ideology becomes necessary to win elections in this system.

But when consensus-driven politics limits freedom of thought, it creates an incentive to curtail individual rights in favor of collective promises. Authoritarian ideologues exploit this by pathologizing dissenters, accusing them of obsession ("the obsession with the veil," "maximalists") or outright madness (sectarian or otherwise).

Ultimately, the question remains: Is freedom the foundation of modern society, or has it become a casualty of ideological control?

30. Patriarchy

Patriarchy: "A form of social organization in which men hold power in political, economic, or religious spheres, or have the dominant role within the family, compared to women."

Patriarchy exists, notably in Islam (Quran 4:34): "Men have authority over women because God has made the one superior to the other, and because they spend their wealth to maintain them."

We will now describe how matriarchy also exists, primarily in the West. Both structures illustrate the challenge of maintaining a balance between Yin and Yang tendencies within human societies. This balance between Yin and Yang is equally beneficial on an individual level. Traditional Chinese medicine defines health as the equilibrium between these forces.

A human being is wealthier than another when they possess more degrees of freedom, all else being equal. Optionality – the ability to choose between different alternatives or life paths – is a mark of both material and spiritual wealth. Signs of poverty, on the other hand, include social determinism and the restriction of one's standard of living to constrained and forced expenditures.

The ultrarich, for instance, are not necessarily "freer" than the upper-middle class. Members of the British royal family, surrounded by their vast wealth, have a near-zero margin of maneuver. They can't vacation on a whim, walk the streets unescorted, or live without the weight of an incessant stream of obligations.

Thus, their degrees of freedom are reduced compared to those of a woman from the upper-middle class, whom we'll call Amanda for this example. Amanda earns a sufficient salary that allows her to live in a pleasant home in a good environment, to hire childcare when she wants, to go on vacations with her children, and, more generally, to enjoy the leisure opportunities available in England. Amanda can live her life fully and freely. We might even consider that not only is the King not wealthier than Amanda, but his life may be less enviable. To truly enjoy his wealth, the King would have to change his social role by exercising his option to abdicate.

Now, let's compare men and women using this framework. Regarding salaries, men seem to have an advantage, with an officially measured average wage gap of about 15%. We can already ask whether the concept of "equal pay for equal work" applies when men and women choose different professions. Does the hardship and danger of a construction site job, where men are the vast majority, compare to that of a bank employee?

Is the amount of time worked the same for men and women, on average? Where are the comparative studies on absenteeism, work accidents, or hours worked? Such studies might reveal differences linked to the fact that women, who more often have custody of children, may have more reasons to be absent or to prefer part-time work. They have the option to work part-time to spend more time raising their children.

Do men have the choice to spend more time with their children? In reality, they are primary parents when it comes to obligations, but second-class when it comes to custody rights after separation (which happens in nearly half of families). Custody is almost always awarded to the mother by family court judges who, in France, are 90% women.

The father is not only deprived of equal rights to see his children but must also financially compensate the mother. In many cases, the mother uses part of this "compensatory payment" to hire a third party to care for the children instead of the father. Yet again, these wealth transfers (not merely income transfers) are conspicuously absent from the statistics, which are constantly presented to reinforce the conspiratorial idea of an alleged systemic patriarchy in modern Western society.

In any case, it's hard to establish that the father still plays "a dominant role within the family" when the justice system and media continually reduce him to a marginal role, if not an ejectable seat, as a parent.

Regarding jobs in large corporations, women often hold key roles in finance, human resources, and communication, allowing them to wield real power without the drawbacks of general management, which is more exposed and subject to dismissal *ad nutum* (at any moment).

For the same reason, women are less likely to engage in the unforgiving game of elections, but those who do often benefit from increased visibility among an electorate that is predominantly female. In 2022, three of the four European institutions were led by women (von der Leyen at the European Commission, Lagarde at the European Central Bank, and Metsola at the European Parliament), but nothing must obstruct the narrative of supposed discrimination against women.

We are constantly reminded that women were denied the right to vote until 1945, but conveniently forgotten is the fact that men were subject to compulsory military service and often forced to die for a system they supposedly controlled. The war in Ukraine serves as a tragic reminder that this discrimination in military obligations persists into the 21st century. Furthermore, the forced labor deportations (euphemistically called *Service du Travail Obligatoire* or *Obligatory Work Service*), imposed by the Vichy government at the behest of the Germans, affected only men—specifically, 650,000 men, 70,000 of whom did not return due to the horrendous working conditions orchestrated by the Nazis.

Why does modern society still insist that the West is a patriarchal system? Especially when its hyperconnected society actually expresses a Yin tendency, by definition of Yin and her inclination toward connection.

It may be an attempt to divert attention so as not to disrupt the victimhood narrative around immigrants. In the political-media orthodoxy, immigrants are seen as bringing to the West a way of life that is not supposed to degrade but enrich our cultural environment. If the immigrant comes from an openly patriarchal culture, any degradation is conveniently downplayed.

David Deida compares the essence of the feminine to the ocean, representing a life force that is uncontrollable and directionless. He associates it with the pursuit of connection and intimacy with others.

For him, the essence of the masculine is the constant pursuit of a goal (purpose).

In energetic terms, the masculine and feminine represent different strategies for reducing entropy: Yin by weaving relationships and Yang by the clarity of his objectives. In other words, the masculine (Yang) seeks freedom and meaning, while the feminine (Yin) seeks love and connections. These tendencies are obviously present in every human being, but not in equal proportions and certainly not equally distributed between the sexes.

When Michel Houellebecq humorously writes in *Plateforme*, "In most circumstances of my life, I have been about as free as a vacuum cleaner," he refers to the suppression of masculinity that has gradually taken hold in Western society. This is why feminists rarely concern themselves with the criteria of freedom, instead focusing their attention on the law, bending it to their will, even to the point of woke ideological tyranny.

Feminists are difficult to satisfy, and it's hard to predict where their demands will end. By definition, an ideology floats above reality and sets no limits. Regarding abortion, they ask for 14 weeks of reflection, even though the law already allows for 12 weeks. In the case of a contraceptive accident, why should it take 14 weeks instead of 12 to decide? If it's a change of mind after a desired pregnancy has begun, it would be appropriate to also consider the father's opinion – unless the father has no rights and only the duty to assume responsibility when the child is born. Under this model, men should show total commitment on demand when a woman decides to have a child and complete detachment when she chooses not to.

Western matriarchy also subtly reshapes ecological discourse. While many have identified the consequences of climate change, opinions diverge on the solutions to adopt. The issue of controlling the world's population, which would primarily involve women in emerging countries, is absent from debates. Among all the forms of restraint being considered, demographic restraint remains taboo, yet it is both the most effective and the least restrictive. Why? Because it would require acknowledging that the burden of restraint falls disproportionately on women in high-birthrate regions. Instead, activists focus on wage equality or access to the circles of power, hitching these causes onto legitimate concerns like violence against women. Achieving a form of social harmony, beyond the sterile opposition between patriarchy and matriarchy, requires recognizing Yin and Yang as distinct and complementary energy flows. True social harmony does not come from eliminating one in favor of the other but from recognizing their distinct roles.

Regarding the definition of Yang, David Deida described it with style: "The path of the man (Yang) is the path of deep gaze, breath, and purpose. It cannot be imitated. The infinite strength of the present is his power and presence. Fear is the lack of trust in the present."

Adherence to Yang leads to behaviors that define a form of assumed masculinity, which involves taking on a sacrificial responsibility to care for a woman, who, in turn, cares for the children. The role of the masculine is to soothe the intrinsic anxiety of the feminine, both sexually and materially, while shaping a desirable future. However, in a dissipative structure as complex as the human species, behaviors must integrate all sorts of social externalities, as material comfort and future prospects themselves depend on exogenous factors.

American essayist Jerr summarizes his masculine vision of the world as follows:

- Emotions are deceptive;
- Life is suffering;
- Life is a game;
- Violence may be necessary;
- Death is certain;
- Do not trust sensations, except hunger;
- Fear nothing, except fear itself

But, according to Jerr, the most appropriate framework for defining the masculine – the expression of Yang in the human species – remains the notion of responsibility. To be masculine is to be responsible. He elaborates:

- Own your failures without blaming others;
- Do not complain;
- Be demanding of yourself;
- If something needs to be done or fixed, do it or fix it;
- Do not ask for permission or seek approval.

The importance of responsibility ranges from the seemingly insignificant, such as mowing the lawn, to the deeply significant, such as promising a woman to care for future children.

Masculinity means taking responsibility for oneself, for others, for the future. Authority naturally comes to those who take responsibility.

Conclusion

God is the name believers give to energy. Like energy, God is invisible, omnipotent, and omnipresent.

The need to dream is embedded in us through evolution. It enabled humanity to endure centuries of slow and continuous progress, lifting us from deprivation and forced simplicity to abundance and comfort. Without this need to believe, without this magical thinking, our ancestors would have likely resigned themselves to their precarious existence and perhaps vanished. Instead, belief united these predators, making them invincible to other species.

Today, the landscape has changed. Proximity has collapsed the vast spaces, and groups now serve both cooperation and division. Magical thinking, once an engine of survival, has become a poison, fueling antagonisms, yet still revered by those who see it as a tool for conquest and the exercise of power.

It is important to remember that our behaviors are influenced, even determined, by the aspiration to reduce entropy and capture maximal energy. The reduction of entropy is expressed through the pursuit of knowledge (Yang) or by seeking connections with the environment (Yin). The more connected a society is, the more it favors Yin, a trait that is emerging in the Western world through the digital transition.

The capture of maximal energy can be understood at the individual level (Yang, competition) and at the collective level (Yin, cooperation), with both the individual and the group being dissipative structures, intertwined by nature. Our well-being depends on the flux of entropy we are capable of producing. When this flux ceases, depression or distress can begin. Hence, we are inclined to accumulate knowledge to reduce our internal entropy, share it to reduce the entropy of our species, and use it to capture more energy.

Yang reduces his entropy by organizing knowledge and establishing connections between ideas and concepts to arrive at solutions for maximizing energy capture. Yang accumulates knowledge through experience and rationality, by gathering evidence and verifying it. Yin, on the other hand, reduces her entropy through human connections, minimizing stress within a superpredator species by developing a belief, forming a group around that belief, and coding the signs of belonging to the group.

In his book *Le Bug Humain*, Sébastien Bohler asks: "The neurons responsible for ensuring our survival are never satisfied and always demand more food, sex, and power. How is it that, despite being aware of this danger, we are unable to react? Can we solve this bug and regain control of our destiny?"

But what Bohler sees as a bug is, in reality, a feature. In reality, the third law of thermodynamics, when applied to humans, doesn't reveal a glitch to be corrected. It reveals a fundamental truth that needs to be accepted. Destiny does not exist, and the pursuit of mastering it is a futile illusion. Collective sobriety, undoubtedly a well-intentioned political goal, conflicts with a fundamental law of physics. The fact that humanity itself is merely a dissipative structure can be seen either as a disenchantment or, conversely, as an invitation to aim for the exceptional, to transcend this modest status.

Humanity appears to be at the crossroads of progress and extinction. But this is an illusion: progress inevitably leads to extinction, which marks the culmination of the evolution of a dissipative structure, reaching the state of maximum entropy. The game is to delay this outcome, which requires rationality and clarity.

Modern humans must navigate between false promises and unpredictability. To close a deal or a negotiation, one must know what can truly be promised. However, anything stemming from a group is uncertain, and anything that doesn't come from a group, like invention or creation, must be exceptional to avoid insignificance.

If culture is a manifestation of the third law, then: "Culture is the rule; art is the exception."

– Jean-Luc Godard

Art and science remain the fields that, through the complexity and depth of their outcomes, distinguish humans from the rest of the living world.

Nihilism is a resignation that overlooks the primary benefit of a scientific education: to elevate us and allow us to happily evolve both in tangible reality and the world of ideas. Science does not offer absolute truths; it offers an evolving framework. It prevents us from settling into a single truth and proclaiming it as certainty, instead inviting us to "offer it shakily as a mystery," as beautifully expressed by the resistant writer Hélie de Saint Marc.

Words are the foundation of a civilized society, capable of coming together to debate ideas rather than clashing over stories and beliefs. But words, when distorted, feed an authoritarian political agenda. Making debate impossible serves first to divide, then to rule without contest. Absurd thinking, where words take on their opposites and where dominance and submission are confused, becomes a mark of recognition for a political-media elite, while discernment is seen as a threat – a risk of exposing the illusion.

Throughout this exploration, we've examined one of the most weaponized anti-concepts (words that complicate rather than facilitate conversations): currency. Through the emblematic lens of anti-concept, we explored the perverse detours taken by the omnipresent and normative communication of the banking lobby.

The modern banking lobby thrives on confusion, using its monopoly to obscure the reality of money. By explaining why credit-created promise-money represents energy supplied by the borrower, not by the issuer, we highlighted the considerable economic advantage granted to banks over other economic actors. In doing so, we opened a debate on the trade-off of the monopoly in terms of service quality and the management of costs borne by the public. We also established that proof-of-work money, materialized by the emergence of the Bitcoin network since 2009, at least offers an alternative that promotes the financing of renewables and methane recovery.

"If you think you've understood what I'm saying, it means I've expressed myself poorly," Alan Greenspan, then director of the U.S. Federal Reserve, once quipped with ironic self-awareness. Yet money, as information representing energy, plays a crucial role in our lives, one that deserves better than being distorted into a regal monopoly to escape debate.

Around terms like "humanity" and "equality," we've seen definitions stretched and distorted to the point of caricature and loss of meaning.

This exploration of the concept of energy through words allowed me to discuss it by alternating between concrete examples and abstraction. I hope it has interested you. And, more importantly, opened a conversation.

Because for you and me, learning never ends.

"If you want to find the secrets of the universe, think in terms of energy, frequency, information, and vibration."

– Nikola Tesla

About the author

Essayist, speaker, and engineer, Pierre Noizat has been dedicated for over ten years to sharing his passion for the science of energy and information.

An independent researcher in the fields of energy, information theory, cryptography, and economics, he offers explanations and solutions based on the connections he draws between these disciplines.

Inspired by Taoism and the legacy of many philosophers and scientists – from Epicurus to Bertrand Russell, including Sadi Carnot and Niels Bohr – his message speaks to those interested in cosmology, economics, and ecology alike.

His book is an inspiring and captivating invitation to explore the science of energy.

Concepts such as potential energy and entropy, the distinction between data and information, and the links between information, currency, and energy will no longer be mysteries to you.

What is commonly known as thermodynamics – a daunting word that evokes dry learning – offers us a new way of seeing reality, enlightened by science and freed from misleading intuitions.

Energy and digital transitions are at the heart of public concerns, yet the physical links between energy and information remain largely unknown.

The principles governing the behavior of energy and information, which explain natural phenomena and social behaviors, are too often overlooked.

Reintroducing rationality into a public debate dominated by ideology requires pedagogy.

After simply restating the three basic principles of thermodynamics, this book illustrates how they apply to our everyday lives through concrete examples.

Bibliography

Ammous, Saifedean. *The Bitcoin Standard : The Decentralized Alternative to Central Banking*. Wiley Publishing, 2018.

Axelrod, Robert. *The Evolution of Cooperation.* Penguin, 1990.

Axelrod, Robert. *The Complexity of Cooperation.* Princeton University Press, 1997.

Balian, Roger. *La longue élaboration du concept d'énergie*. Académie des sciences, 2013.

Boehm, Christopher. *Hierarchy in the forest.* Harvard University Press, 1999.

Bouveresse, Jacques. *Déterminisme et causalité, Les Études philosophiques*, vol. 58, no. 3, 2001.

Chomsky Noam, Herman Edward. *Manufacturing Consent, the Political Economy of the Mass Media*. Pantheon Books, 1988.

Dewar, Roderick. *Information theory explanation of the fluctuation theorem.* IOP Publishing, 2003.

Dyer, Wayne. *Your Sacred Self*, William Morrow, 1994.

Gauchet, Marcel. *The Disenchantment of the World: A Political History of Religion.* Princeton University Press, 1997.

Graeber, David. *Debt : The First 5000 Years.* Melville House, 2011.

Harari, Yuval Noah. *Sapiens : A Brief History of Humankind.* Harper, 2014.

Houellebecq, Michel. *Whatever, a novel.* Serpent's Tail, 1998

Hülsmann, Jörg Guido. *The Ethics of Money Production.* Mises Institute, 2018.

Huntington, Samuel. *Qui sommes-nous ? Identité nationale et choc des cultures.* Odile Jacob, 2004.

John Dominik. *Can We Reverse Time? Entropy And The Time-Flips in Your Morning Coffee.* Medium.com, 2025

Martyushev L.M., Seleznev V.D. « *Maximum entropy production principle in physics, chemistry and biology* ». Physics Reports, Volume 426, Issue 1, 2006.

Mihelich, Martin. « *Vers une compréhension du principe de maximisation de production d'entropie* ». Physique mathématique. Université Paris Saclay (COmUE), 2015.

Perry, John. *Identity, Personal Identity, and the Self*. Hackett, 2002.

Popper, Karl. *The Open Society and Its Enemies*. Routledge, 1945.

Popper, Karl. *The Logic of Scientific Discovery*. Julius Springer, Hutchinson & Co, 1959.

Prigogine, Ilya. *La fin des certitudes. Temps, chaos et les lois de la nature*. Odile Jacob, 1996.

Putnam, Robert. *Bowling Alone, The Collapse and Revival of American Community*. Simon & Schuster, 2000.

Russell, Bertrand. *Religion and Science*. Thornton Butterworth, 1935

Smil, Vaclav. *Energy and Civilization*. MIT Press, 2017.

Sneddon IN Hill R Naghdi PM Ziegler H. « *Progress in Solid Mechanics. Vol. 4* ». North-Holland Publishing Company ; John Wiley & Sons ; 1963.

Zweig, Stefan. *Die unsichtbare sammlung*. Halcyon-presse, 1933

Glossary & notes

Anthropocene

Anthropocene is a proposed geological period marking when human influence on the planet and its ecosystems became significant.

The term Anthropocene, meaning "era of the humans," was popularized by 1995 Nobel Prize-winning chemist Paul Josef Crutzen and biologist Eugene Stoermer.

They suggest the Anthropocene began in the late 18th century with the Industrial Revolution, directly following the Holocene.

Dharma

In its Buddhist definition, Dharma refers to the everlasting, common truth expressed by Buddha. Dharma, Buddha, and the Sanga, the community of Buddhist practitioners, comprise the Triratna, or "three jewels."

In Buddhist metaphysics, the plural form, the dharmas, means the interconnected components of the empiric world. One key takeaway of this book is that all the components of our observable universe are interdependent since they are all different forms of the same natural force: energy.

(Note: Dharma has distinct meanings in Hinduism and Jainism, which are beyond the scope of this book.)

Free energy

This expression designates energy in a form that is relatively easy to transform into work. For example, electricity is a form of free energy since it can be efficiently transformed into work by an electric engine.

Homeostasis

In biology and thermodynamics, homeostasis is a self-organization principle by which a system maintains a key parameter. Temperature, for example, is maintained near a certain value.

As a dissipative structure deals with a varying inflow of energy, homeostasis ensures that energy is relatively evenly distributed within the structure. Homeostasis allows the dissipative structure to adapt to small, rapid variations of the energy inflow, much like evolution is an adaptation to large, long-term variations.

Lightning

The Lightning network is to the Bitcoin network what Visa/Mastercard networks are to traditional bank payment systems. In other words, the Lightning network conveys payment authorization messages that are subsequently aggregated and executed on the Bitcoin network.

As Bastien Teinturier, CTO of Acinq, a company specializing in Lightning network technology, explains:

> Two users, Alice and Bob, start by opening a bidirectionnal payment channel between themselves, each user commiting a funding Bitcoin transaction. Alice and Bob can then send and receive bitcoins within this newly opened payment channel. They create and sign a transaction that describes the new balance of the funds on the channels. They do not broadcast the transaction on the Bitcoin network yet so they can replace it with a new one each time they decide to trade between each other. Only when they publish the final transaction on the Bitcoin network, the Lightning payment channel is closed. Lightning payments are peer-to-peer and Alice and Bob are in control of their financial data privacy.

The Lightning network scales the Bitcoin network by enabling millions of transactions per second via off-chain payment channels. In this context, the Bitcoin network is then used only to open and close these channels, making it a settlement layer rather than a transaction processor for every payment.

Pool mining

In Bitcoin, the chance of a miner successfully adding the next block to the blockchain is proportional to their share of the total network computing power. For example, a miner that controls 0.02 % of the computing power would wait on average 5000 blocks, i.e., 35 days, before validating a new block. Since it is a probabilistic process, the miner could wait several months before receiving a block reward. Therefore, to receive a steadier flow of income, miners tend to join cooperative groups that pool the computing power of the participants and reward them according to their contribution to the pool.

Photon

A particle, quantum of energy: a flow of photons forms an electromagnetic radiation.

Dissipative structure

An open system, receiving a flow of energy, transforming part of it into free energy, dissipating the rest as heat.

Notes on Taoïsm

Taoïsm is a Chinese philosophy inspired by the Tao Te Ching (a book also known as *Daodejing* or *Tao-tö-king*, in Chinese 道德经, in English, the book of the Path and Virtue), a classic text transcribing the thoughts of Lao Tzu around 500 BC.

In this book, I use the concepts of Yin and Yang as symbols representing the polar dimension of energy. For example, the spin of an elementary particle is an expression of this polarity at the quantum level, while sexual differentiation of living beings expresses it at the macroscopic level.

Importantly, my use of these symbols does not imply a vindication of the mysticism in the religious tradition. I believe that Lao Tzu is a philosopher, like Buddha, or a group of philosophers, but certainly not a god.

Yin and Yang

- *Yin* (陰 / 阴), represented in black, is associated with the feminine, the moon, darkness, the earth, cold, autumn, receptivity, and connection. Feminine Yin aims to connect to her environment and to share information.
- Yang (陽 / 阳), represented in white, is linked to the masculine, the sun, light, the sky, heat, spring, action, and control. Masculine Yang aims to control his environment and to find information.

Yin and Yang are not rigid stereotypes but rather interpretive tools that help us understand the emotional patterns and behaviors that form individual character. Yang is associated with activation energy, while Yin carries the hidden potential of transformation.

Yin/Yang key pairs:

Earth/sky, autumn/spring, winter/summer, night/day, stock/flow, feminine/masculine, younger/older, misery/success, even/odd, silence/speech, receiving/giving, student/teacher.

The Yin/Yang symbols meant so much to Niels Bohr, the physicist who developed the atom model that led to significant advancement in quantum physics, that he adopted them as his blazon, coat of arms. Bohr also introduced the concept of complementarity that can be illustrated by the yin-yang symbols: quantum physics must admit pairs of descriptions that can be contradictory, like the dual wave/particle description of the photon.

This principle mirrors the Taoist embrace of paradox and was a response to the apparent impossibility of a unified, complete understanding of phenomena at quantum levels. In quantum physics, contradictions often arise not from the phenomena themselves but from the perspective taken by the observer.

Notes on Gramsci

"One must balance the pessimism of intelligence with the optimism of will."

This motto, attributed to the philosopher Antonio Gramsci, resonates strongly with our times.

Gramsci's key contribution is rooted in his theory of *cultural hegemony*, which is the idea that power is maintained not only through political or economic control but by shaping public consciousness. He argued that the ruling class secures its dominance by influencing cultural norms, values, and beliefs, embedding its worldview into everyday life.

Gramsci emphasized how collective habits, institutions, and ideologies reinforce systems of control, making them appear natural or inevitable. True change, in his view, requires more than just seizing political power; it must reshape the cultural landscape that legitimizes it.

Notes on hashrate

The computing power of a proof-of-work network can be measured by the number of hashes computed per second, using the following units:

GH/s (*gigahash*)	1 000 000 000
TH/s (*terahash*)	1 000 000 000 000
PH/s (*petahash*)	1 000 000 000 000 000
EH/s (*exahash*)	1 000 000 000 000 000 000
ZH/s (*zettahash*)	1 000 000 000 000 000 000 000
YH/s (*yottahash*)	1 000 000 000 000 000 000 000 000

Every computed hash means one attempt to find a value of the hash function (for example, SHA256 in the Bitcoin protocol) that is below the target set by the mining protocol.

NOTES

1. According to the Cambridge dictionary, a polymath is a person who knows a lot about many different subjects.
2. Pascal M., de Crouy Chanel P., Wagner V., Corso M., Tillier C., Bentayeb M., Blanchard M., Cochet A., Pascal L., Host S., Goria S., Le Tertre A., Chatignoux E., Ung A., Beaudeau P., Medina S. (2016b). The mortality impacts of fine particles in France. Science of the Total Environment 571, 416-25
3. The law of diminishing returns states that when a variable factor of production is added to some fixed factors of production, the marginal product (MP) initially increases but eventually diminishes.
4. Negentropy is defined as the difference between the entropy of a system and the maximum possible entropy of the same system.
5. https://assets.pewresearch.org/wp-content/uploads/sites/11/2017/04/07092755/FULL-REPORT-WITH-APPENDIXES-A-AND-B-APRIL-3.pdf
6. https://ncase.me/fireflies/
7. World - Major Central Bank M2 Money Supply: https://en.macromicro.me/series/4675/global-money-supply-m2
8. As of mid-February 2024, the market cap of Bitcoin exceeded 1,000 billion US dollars.
9. World Population Prospects 2019
10. BCG, The New Growth Game,Global Payments Report 2022.
11. See, Lightning Network in glossary.
12. See, Pool Mining in glossary.
13. https://news.un.org/fr/story/2022/01/1112132
14. https://coindoo.com/scrypt-asic-vs-sha-256-crypto-mining-hardware-comparison/
15. coinmarketcap.com on March 1, 2024
16. The Laffer Curve illustrates the idea that lower tax rates can lead to increased

government revenue by encouraging businesses to invest and operate within the country. According to this theory, reducing taxes can positively influence economic behavior and stimulate growth. (*Source: Cambridge Dictionary*)

17. https://www.ebf.eu/wp-content/uploads/2022/01/FINAL-Banking-in-Europe-EBF-Facts-and-Figures-2021.-11-January-2022.pdf

18. https://ec.europa.eu/eurostat/statistics-explained/index.php?title=Tertiary_education_statistics#Teaching_staff

www.ingramcontent.com/pod-product-compliance
Lightning Source LLC
LaVergne TN
LVHW040518210926
848480LV00007BA/1500

* 9 7 8 9 9 1 6 7 4 9 6 4 7 *